EXPLORING C+
FROM BEGINNER TO
ADVANCED

Learn C++ Programming from Scratch and Master Object-Oriented Programming for Building Fast, Efficient Software

Author: LINSEL TADASHI

1ST EDITION

TABLE OF CONTENTS

ABOUT THE AUTHOR!

Linsel Tadashi (Author)

Linsel Tadashi is a seasoned technology expert with deep expertise in software engineering, system architecture, and digital innovation. With a career spanning years of developing and optimizing high-performance solutions, he has worked with top global tech firms to drive technological advancements. Linsel is widely recognized for his ability to simplify intricate technical concepts, making them accessible to developers and industry professionals alike. His passion for cutting-edge technology, coupled with his forward-thinking approach to problem-solving, has positioned him as a respected mentor and thought leader in the tech community.

CHAPTER 1: INTRODUCTION TO EXPLORING C++

Welcome & Why C++?

Welcome to the world of C++ programming! Whether you're a complete beginner taking your first steps into coding, a hobbyist eager to build efficient software, or a professional looking to refine your skills, you've picked an excellent language to begin your journey. In this section, we'll explore the significance of C++, discuss why it remains one of the most popular programming languages in the world, and set the stage for the exciting material ahead.

1.1 The Legacy and Power of C++

C++ is a multi-paradigm programming language that combines the performance and efficiency of low-level languages with the expressiveness of high-level languages. Developed in the early 1980s by Bjarne Stroustrup, C++ was designed to build systems where resource efficiency and performance are paramount. Today, C++ is used in domains as diverse as game development, embedded systems, high-frequency trading, and even scientific computing.

Key Benefits of C++:

Performance: C++ allows you to write programs that run quickly and use system resources efficiently. Its compiled nature and fine control over memory and system resources make it an excellent choice for performance-critical applications.

Flexibility: With support for both procedural and object-oriented programming, C++ gives you the tools to tackle virtually any type of programming challenge.

Control: Unlike many higher-level languages, C++ offers direct control over hardware and memory, making it ideal for applications where low-level manipulation is necessary.

Community and Ecosystem: With decades of development, an extensive ecosystem of libraries and tools, and a large community of experts, C++ offers plenty of resources to help you overcome challenges and accelerate your learning.

Imagine C++ as the engine behind a high-performance sports car—robust, powerful, and capable of delivering exceptional speed and precision when tuned correctly. As you progress through this book, you'll learn how to build that engine from scratch, step by step.

1.2 Why Should You Learn C++?

Understanding why you should learn C++ can be the first spark that motivates your journey. Here are a few reasons why C++ is a worthwhile investment of your time:

Industry Relevance: C++ remains the backbone of many critical applications in industries like finance, gaming, telecommunications, and aerospace. By learning C++, you're positioning yourself to work on projects that demand the highest performance.

Career Growth: Mastering C++ can open doors to advanced programming roles, including system development, game development, and even research positions in computer science.

Problem-Solving Skills: The language's complexity encourages a deep understanding of computer architecture and algorithms, which are invaluable skills for any programmer.

Foundation for Other Languages: Learning C++ provides a solid foundation in programming concepts such as memory management, object-oriented design, and generic programming, all of which can be applied to other languages.

Throughout this book, we'll not only explain how to write C++ code but also delve into the "why" behind the techniques, ensuring you gain a deep understanding of the language's underlying principles.

1.3 Setting the Tone for the Journey Ahead

Our goal is to make your learning experience engaging, practical, and enjoyable. We've structured this book so that each chapter builds on the last, gradually moving from simple concepts to more advanced techniques. Think of this book as a guided tour through the expansive world of C++ programming, where you'll have plenty of hands-on projects, real-world examples, and expert tips along the way.

Before we dive deeper into the core concepts of C++, take a moment to reflect on what you hope to achieve. Whether your goal is to build your own applications, contribute to open-source projects, or simply understand how modern software works, this book will provide you with the skills and confidence needed to succeed.

2: Core Concepts and Theory

In this section, we'll explore the fundamental concepts that underpin C++ programming. Our discussion will be structured around a few key ideas that you'll encounter repeatedly as you progress: compiled languages, static typing, memory management, and object-oriented programming. By understanding these core concepts, you'll gain the theoretical foundation that makes writing efficient C++ code possible.

2.1 Compiled Languages vs. Interpreted Languages

C++ is a compiled language. This means that the code you write is translated by a compiler into machine code that your computer can execute directly. Let's break down the implications of this process:

Compilation: When you write a C++ program, you save your code in a source file (with a .cpp extension). A compiler (such as GCC, Clang, or MSVC) then translates this source code into an executable file. This process involves several steps including preprocessing, compiling, assembling, and linking.

Efficiency: Because C++ code is compiled directly into machine code, it generally runs much faster than interpreted code. This is one reason why C++ is often chosen for performance-critical applications.

Error Detection: Compilation also provides an early opportunity to catch syntax and type errors before the program is run, which can save time in the debugging process.

Analogy:
Think of compiling C++ code as baking a cake from a recipe. The recipe (source code) is transformed into a finished cake (executable) through a series of steps (preprocessing, compiling, linking). Just as the quality of a cake depends on following the recipe and using the right ingredients, the performance of your program depends on the quality of your code and the efficiency of the compiler.

2.2   Static   Typing   and   Memory Management

C++ is a statically typed language, meaning that the type of every variable is known at compile time. This offers several advantages:

Type Safety: Errors related to data types are caught early, reducing bugs in your program.

Performance: Knowing variable types at compile time allows the compiler to optimize memory usage and execution speed.

Readability: Explicit type declarations help document your code, making it easier to understand and maintain.

Example:

cpp

int age = 30;

double salary = 55000.50;

In the snippet above, the type of each variable is declared explicitly, ensuring that operations involving these variables are performed correctly.

Memory management is another cornerstone of C++. Unlike some languages that handle memory automatically, C++ gives you direct control over memory allocation and deallocation. This control can lead to highly optimized code but also requires careful management to avoid issues like memory leaks or dangling pointers.

Key Points on Memory Management:

Stack vs. Heap: Variables declared inside functions are stored on the stack, while dynamic memory (allocated using new or malloc) is stored on the heap.

Manual Control: You must explicitly release dynamically allocated memory using delete or free.

Performance Considerations: While manual memory management can improve performance, it also introduces complexity. Learning best practices in memory management early on will save you a great deal of trouble later.

2.3 The Paradigm of Object-Oriented Programming (OOP)

Object-oriented programming is central to C++. OOP is based on the idea of "objects" – entities that combine data and behavior. The primary principles of OOP include:

Encapsulation: Bundling data with methods that operate on that data.

Inheritance: Allowing new classes to inherit properties and methods from existing classes.

Polymorphism: Enabling objects to be treated as instances of their parent class rather than their actual class.

Real-World Example:

Imagine a car manufacturing company. Each car (object) has properties such as color, engine size, and model, as well as behaviors such as accelerating, braking, and honking. By defining a "Car" class in C++, you can encapsulate these properties and behaviors, and then create multiple car objects that share the same structure but have different attribute values.

2.4 The Role of the Standard Template Library (STL)

C++ comes with a rich set of libraries that extend its functionality, the most important of which is the Standard Template Library (STL). The STL provides ready-to-use classes and functions for data structures and algorithms. Key components include:

Containers: Data structures such as vectors, lists, and maps.

Algorithms: Functions for searching, sorting, and manipulating data.

Iterators: Objects that allow traversal through container elements.

2.5 Putting It All Together

Let's look at a simple example that combines these core concepts. Consider a program that creates a list of numbers, sorts them, and prints the sorted list. This example will demonstrate compilation, static typing, memory management, and the use of the STL.

Example Code:

```cpp
cpp
#include <iostream>
#include <vector>
#include <algorithm> // For std::sort

using namespace std;

int main() (
    // Create a vector (dynamic array) of integers
    vector<int> numbers = (42, 7, 19, 73, 5);

    // Sort the vector in ascending order
    sort(numbers.begin(), numbers.end());

    // Display the sorted numbers
    cout << "Sorted numbers: ";
    for (int num : numbers) (
        cout << num << " ";
    )
    cout << endl;
```

```
return 0;
)
```

Explanation:

Compilation & Static Typing: The code is compiled and every variable is explicitly typed.

STL Usage: We use a vector to store the numbers and the STL's sort algorithm to order them.

Memory Management: Although we don't allocate dynamic memory manually here, understanding that STL containers handle memory internally is key.

By grasping these core concepts, you're well on your way to understanding why C++ is both powerful and versatile. In the next sections, we'll build upon these fundamentals by showing you how to set up your development environment and write your first simple programs.

3: Tools and Setup

Before you start writing C++ code, it's important to set up your development environment correctly. In this section, we'll cover everything you need to know about the tools and platforms that will form the backbone of your coding journey. We'll guide you through choosing an editor or IDE, installing the necessary compilers, and configuring your system for a smooth development experience.

3.1 Choosing an IDE or Text Editor

An Integrated Development Environment (IDE) can simplify the coding process by offering features like code completion, debugging tools, and project management. Here are a few popular choices for C++ development:

Visual Studio (Windows):

A powerful IDE from Microsoft, ideal for Windows development. It offers an intuitive interface, a robust debugger, and many built-in tools for code analysis.

CLion (Cross-Platform):

Developed by JetBrains, CLion is a cross-platform IDE that supports C++ development with smart code assistance, refactoring tools, and a built-in debugger.

Code::Blocks (Cross-Platform):

A free, open-source IDE that is lightweight and highly customizable. It's a great option for beginners.

Visual Studio Code (VS Code):

A versatile text editor that, when paired with the right extensions, becomes a powerful environment for C++ development.

Tip:
If you're just starting out, choose an IDE that suits your operating system and personal preferences. For instance, Visual Studio is an excellent choice for Windows users, while VS Code offers flexibility across platforms.

3.2 Installing a Compiler

C++ requires a compiler to convert your source code into an executable program. Below are instructions for installing a compiler on various platforms:

Windows – Installing MinGW (GCC)

Download MinGW:

Visit the MinGW website and download the installer.

Install MinGW:

Follow the installer's instructions to set up the GCC compiler on your machine.

Configure Environment Variables:

Add the MinGW bin directory to your system's PATH. This allows you to compile C++ programs from the command line.

Example (Command Prompt):

```shell
set PATH=%PATH%;C:\MinGW\bin
```

macOS – Installing Xcode Command Line Tools

Open Terminal:

Launch Terminal from your Applications folder.

Install Tools:

Run the following command:

```shell
xcode-select --install
```

Verify Installation:

Once installed, you can verify by typing:

```shell
gcc --version
```

Linux - Installing GCC

On most Linux distributions, GCC is available through the package manager. For example, on Ubuntu:

```shell
sudo apt update
sudo apt install build-essential
```

3.3 Configuring Your Environment

Once your IDE and compiler are installed, configuring your environment for C++ development is essential. Here are some steps to ensure a smooth setup:

Project Structure:

Organize your projects with a clear folder structure. For example:

css

```
MyCppProjects/
├── Project1_HelloWorld/
│      └── main.cpp
└── Project2_Calculator/
       └── main.cpp
```

This helps keep your code organized and easily navigable.

Editor Settings:

Customize your IDE's settings—such as theme, font size, and indentation rules—to make coding more comfortable. Most IDEs allow you to import or export these settings for consistency across projects.

Version Control:

Consider using Git to manage your code. Even as a beginner, learning basic version control will help you track changes and collaborate with others. Install Git and create a GitHub account to store your projects online.

3.4 Verifying Your Setup

Before moving on, it's important to verify that everything is working correctly. Let's create a simple "Hello, World!" program to test our setup.

Example Code:

```cpp
#include <iostream>

using namespace std;

int main() (
    cout << "Hello, World!" << endl;
    return 0;
)
```

Step-by-Step Instructions:

Open your IDE or text editor and create a new file named main.cpp.

 the code snippet above into your file.

Save the file and compile it using your chosen method (e.g., through the IDE's build button or via command line with g++ main.cpp -o hello).

Run the resulting executable. You should see the message "Hello, World!" printed on the screen.

By completing these steps, you'll confirm that your development environment is ready for more complex projects.

4: Hands-on Examples & Projects

In this section, we'll put theory into practice with a series of hands-on examples and projects. Each project is designed to reinforce the concepts introduced earlier and to build your confidence as you start writing and running C++ code. We'll start with a very basic "Hello, World!" program, then move on to slightly more complex projects that illustrate core C++ features.

4.1 Project 1: Your First C++ Program – "Hello, World!"

4.1.1 Overview

The "Hello, World!" program is the traditional first step in learning any new programming language. Its simplicity allows you to focus on the process of writing, compiling, and executing code without getting bogged down in complex logic.

4.1.2 Step-by-Step Walkthrough

Creating the Source File:

Open your IDE or text editor.

Create a new file and name it main.cpp.

Writing the Code:

```cpp
#include <iostream>  // Preprocessor directive to include
input-output stream library

// The main function is the entry point of any C++ program.
int main() (
```

```
    std::cout << "Hello, World!" << std::endl; // Print message
to the console
    return 0; // Exit the program successfully
)
```

Code Explanation:

#include <iostream> tells the compiler to include the standard input/output stream library.

The main() function is where the program begins execution.

std::cout is used to print text to the console.

std::endl ends the line, ensuring that the output is neatly formatted.

Compiling the Code:

In your IDE, press the "Build" or "Compile" button.

If using the command line, type:

```shell
g++ main.cpp -o HelloWorld
```

This command compiles main.cpp and creates an executable named HelloWorld.

Running the Program:

In the IDE, click the "Run" button.

From the command line:

```shell
./HelloWorld
```

You should see the output:

Hello, World!

4.1.3 Visual Walkthrough

Diagram: "Hello, World!" Flow

Step 1: Create main.cpp

Step 2: Write code

Step 3: Compile → Executable

Step 4: Run → Output: "Hello, World!"

This diagram (Figure 4) visually represents the process from writing code to executing the program.

4.2 Project 2: Building a Simple Calculator

4.2.1 Overview

For our second project, we'll create a simple calculator. This project will introduce you to variables, basic arithmetic operations, and user input in C++. The calculator will be able to perform addition, subtraction, multiplication, and division.

4.2.2 Code Walkthrough

Creating the Source File:

Create a new file named calculator.cpp.

Writing the Code:

```cpp
#include <iostream>

using namespace std;

int main() {
    double num1, num2;
    char op;
    cout << "Enter first number: ";
    cin >> num1;
    cout << "Enter an operator (+, -, *, /): ";
```

```cpp
cin >> op;
cout << "Enter second number: ";
cin >> num2;

switch(op) {
    case '+':
        cout << "Result: " << num1 + num2 << endl;
        break;
    case '-':
        cout << "Result: " << num1 - num2 << endl;
        break;
    case '*':
        cout << "Result: " << num1 * num2 << endl;
        break;
    case '/':
        if (num2 != 0)
            cout << "Result: " << num1 / num2 << endl;
        else
            cout << "Error: Division by zero!" << endl;
        break;
    default:
        cout << "Invalid operator!" << endl;
}

    return 0;
}
```

Code Explanation:

We include the <iostream> library to handle input/output.

The program prompts the user to enter two numbers and an operator.

The switch statement selects the appropriate arithmetic operation based on the operator input.

Error handling is demonstrated with a check for division by zero.

Compiling and Running:

Compile with:

```shell
g++ calculator.cpp -o Calculator
```

Run the executable:

```shell
./Calculator
```

Follow the on-screen prompts to perform calculations.

4.2.3 Project Enhancements

To make your calculator more robust, consider adding the following features:

Input Validation: Check that the user enters valid numbers and operators.

Looping: Allow the user to perform multiple calculations in one run.

Function Decomposition: Break the program into functions (e.g., one function per arithmetic operation) to make the code cleaner and more modular.

Input: User enters two numbers and an operator.

Processing: switch statement determines the operation.

Output: Result is displayed.

4.3 Project 3: Environment Verification Tool

4.3.1 Overview

An often-overlooked but critical project is an environment verification tool. This project will help you confirm that your C++ development environment is properly configured. It will perform several checks and print detailed information about the compiler, system, and available libraries.

4.3.2 Code Walkthrough

Creating the Source File:

Create a file named env_check.cpp.

Writing the Code:

```cpp
#include <iostream>
#include <cstdlib>

using namespace std;

// Function to display compiler information using
preprocessor macros
void displayCompilerInfo() (
    cout << "Compiler Information:" << endl;
#ifdef __clang__
    cout << " Compiler: Clang" << endl;
#elif defined(__GNUC__)
    cout << " Compiler: GCC" << endl;
#elif defined(_MSC_VER)
    cout << " Compiler: MSVC" << endl;
#else
    cout << " Compiler: Unknown" << endl;
#endif
)
// Function to check if the operating system is supported
void displayOSInfo() (
#if defined(_WIN32)
    cout << "Operating System: Windows" << endl;
#elif defined(__APPLE__) || defined(__MACH__)
    cout << "Operating System: macOS" << endl;
#elif defined(__linux__)
    cout << "Operating System: Linux" << endl;
#else
    cout << "Operating System: Unknown" << endl;
#endif
)
```

```cpp
int main() {
    cout << "Environment Verification Tool" << endl;
    cout << "-----------------------------" << endl;

    displayCompilerInfo();
    displayOSInfo();

    // Check for common environment variables (example: PATH)
    char* path = std::getenv("PATH");
    if (path != nullptr) {
        cout << "PATH variable: " << path << endl;
    } else {
        cout << "PATH variable is not set!" << endl;
    }

    cout << "Environment setup appears to be complete." << endl;
    return 0;
}
```

Code Explanation:

The program uses preprocessor macros to determine the compiler and operating system.

It then retrieves the PATH environment variable to confirm that it's set correctly.

This tool is particularly useful for verifying that your environment is ready for more advanced projects.

Compiling and Running:

Compile with:

```shell
g++ env_check.cpp -o EnvCheck
```

Run the tool:

```shell
./EnvCheck
```

4.3.3 Extending the Tool

As you become more comfortable, extend this tool to:

Check the versions of libraries or tools (e.g., Git, CMake).

Log the environment information to a file for future reference.

Provide recommendations if certain expected tools or libraries are missing.

Start: Run the tool.

Check: Compiler info, OS info, environment variables.

Output: Display environment status.

4.4 Best Practices in Project Development

Throughout these projects, keep the following best practices in mind:

Comment Your Code:

Always include comments that explain what each part of your code does. This makes it easier to understand when you revisit your projects later.

Use Meaningful Variable Names:

Choose variable names that clearly describe their purpose. For example, instead of naming a variable x, use userInput or result.

Break Down Problems:

Divide larger projects into smaller, manageable functions or modules. This not only makes the code easier to debug but also improves readability.

Test Frequently:

Compile and run your code often to catch errors early. Use simple test cases to ensure that each component of your project works as expected.

Seek Feedback:

Don't hesitate to share your code with peers or online communities. Feedback can help you refine your skills and adopt best practices.

Each project in this section builds on the previous one, gradually increasing in complexity. By the end of this section, you'll have created several practical applications that not only reinforce your understanding of C++ fundamentals but also prepare you for more advanced programming challenges.

5: Advanced Techniques & Optimization

Even in an introductory chapter, it's valuable to touch on advanced techniques that can improve your code and environment setup. In this section, we'll explore some optimization strategies and advanced techniques that you can use even in simple projects to make your code more efficient and maintainable.

5.1 Advanced Compiler Flags and Optimizations

Modern compilers offer a range of optimization flags that can significantly improve your program's performance. For example, the GCC compiler includes flags like -O2 and -O3 that enable aggressive optimizations.

Example Command:

shell

g++ -O2 main.cpp -o OptimizedHelloWorld

Explanation:

-O2: Enables a good balance of performance improvements without significantly increasing compile time.

-O3: Applies even more aggressive optimizations that can further improve speed but might also increase the size of the executable or expose subtle bugs.

Trade-offs:
Aggressive optimizations can sometimes make debugging more difficult, as the code structure may be transformed. It's best to use these optimizations once you are confident that your code is stable.

5.2 Using Debuggers and Profilers

A powerful debugger is an essential tool in any programmer's toolkit. For C++ development, tools like GDB (GNU Debugger) and built-in IDE debuggers help you step through your code, inspect variables, and find logical errors.

Example: Using GDB

Compile your code with the -g flag to include debugging information:

```shell
g++ -g main.cpp -o DebugHelloWorld
```

Start GDB:

```shell
gdb DebugHelloWorld
```

Set breakpoints, run your program, and step through code to inspect the state.

5.3 Code Refactoring and Modularization

As you build larger projects, organizing your code becomes critical. Refactoring your code to improve readability and maintainability is an advanced technique that pays off in the long run.

Tips for Effective Refactoring:

Modularize: Break your code into functions and classes.

Consistent Naming: Use consistent and descriptive naming conventions.

Documentation: Maintain clear documentation and inline comments.

Example Refactoring: Before:

```cpp
#include <iostream>
using namespace std;


int main() (
```

```cpp
    int a, b;
    cout << "Enter two numbers: ";
    cin >> a >> b;
    cout << "Sum: " << a + b << endl;
    return 0;
)
```

After (with a separate function):

```cpp
cpp
#include <iostream>
using namespace std;

int addNumbers(int x, int y) (
    return x + y;
)

int main() (
    int a, b;
    cout << "Enter two numbers: ";
    cin >> a >> b;
    cout << "Sum: " << addNumbers(a, b) << endl;
    return 0;
)
```

5.4 Leveraging External Libraries

While the Standard Template Library (STL) is powerful, there are many third-party libraries available for C++ that can help you solve complex problems with minimal code. Examples include Boost for advanced data structures and algorithms, and OpenCV for computer vision applications.

Example: Integrating a Third-Party Library Imagine you need to perform complex string manipulations. The Boost Library offers extensive support for this. Here's a simple example using Boost's string algorithms:

```cpp
cpp
#include <boost/algorithm/string.hpp>
```

```cpp
#include <iostream>
#include <vector>

using namespace std;

int main() {
    string data = "C++ is powerful and efficient!";
    vector<string> words;
    boost::split(words, data, boost::is_any_of(" "));

    for (const auto& word : words)
        cout << word << endl;

    return 0;
}
```

Note: To compile code using Boost, you may need to install the library and configure your project accordingly.

5.5 Performance Optimization Tips

Beyond compiler optimizations, here are some advanced techniques to improve performance:

Efficient Data Structures: Choose the right data structure for the job. For instance, use std::vector for dynamic arrays, but consider std::deque or std::list if you need frequent insertions and deletions.

Avoid Unnecessary Copies: Use references or move semantics to avoid ing large objects.

Memory Management: Use smart pointers (like std::unique_ptr and std::shared_ptr) to manage dynamic memory safely and efficiently.

Inline Functions: For small, frequently called functions, consider inlining to reduce function call overhead.

By adopting these advanced techniques, you'll be better prepared to write code that not only works but works efficiently. Even if you don't implement these optimizations immediately, being aware of them will help you make informed decisions as you progress in your C++ journey.

6: Troubleshooting and Problem-Solving

No learning journey is without its bumps. In this section, we'll address some common challenges that beginners face when setting up their environment or writing their first C++ programs. We'll provide practical troubleshooting tips, debugging advice, and solutions to common error messages.

6.1 Common Setup Issues

6.1.1 Compiler Not Found

If you encounter an error indicating that the compiler is not found, ensure that:

The compiler is installed (e.g., MinGW for Windows, Xcode for macOS, build-essential for Linux).

Your system's PATH environment variable includes the compiler's binary directory.

Troubleshooting Tip:

Open a command prompt or terminal and type:

shell

g++ --version

If the command isn't recognized, double-check your installation and PATH settings.

6.1.2 Missing Libraries or Headers

Sometimes your code might fail to compile because the compiler cannot find necessary header files. This is often due to misconfigured include paths or missing library installations.

Solution:
Ensure that your development environment is set up to include standard libraries and any third-party libraries you're using. Consult your IDE's documentation on configuring include directories.

6.2 Debugging Syntax and Runtime Errors

6.2.1 Syntax Errors

Syntax errors are among the most common issues when you're just starting out. The compiler typically provides a line number and a description of the error. Read these messages carefully—they often tell you exactly what's wrong.

Example Error Message:

kotlin

error: 'cout' was not declared in this scope

Solution:
Make sure you include the correct header:

cpp

#include <iostream>

using namespace std;

6.2.2 Runtime Errors and Crashes

Runtime errors, such as segmentation faults or division by zero, occur while your program is running. Use debugging tools like GDB to trace the source of these errors.

Debugging Steps:

Compile your code with the -g flag to include debugging symbols.

Run your program in GDB and set breakpoints.

Step through your code and inspect variables to identify where the error occurs.

6.3 Troubleshooting Environment Configuration

Even with careful setup, you might run into issues related to your development environment. Here are some common problems and solutions:

Issue: IDE fails to detect the compiler.

Solution: Verify that the compiler's executable is in the system PATH and that your IDE is configured to use the correct toolchain.

Issue: Conflicting versions of libraries.

Solution: Check that all components (compiler, IDE, libraries) are compatible. If necessary, update or downgrade components to resolve version conflicts.

Issue: Slow compile times.

Solution: Use compiler optimization flags judiciously during development, and disable them when debugging to speed up the iterative process.

Before-and-After Code Example: Debugging a Common Issue

Before:

```cpp
#include <iostream>

int main() {
    int num;
    std::cout << "Enter a number: ";
    std::cin >> num;
    std::cout << "You entered: " << num << std::endl;
    return 0;
}
```

After adding proper namespace declaration:

```cpp
#include <iostream>
using namespace std;

int main() {
    int num;
    cout << "Enter a number: ";
    cin >> num;
    cout << "You entered: " << num << endl;
    return 0;
```

)

This small change resolved the issue of undefined references to cout and cin.

6.4 Developing a Problem-Solving Mindset

Troubleshooting isn't just about fixing errors—it's also about developing a systematic approach to solving problems:

Read the Error Messages Carefully: They often contain clues that lead directly to the solution.

Break Down the Problem: Isolate the code causing the error by commenting out sections or using test cases.

Use Online Resources: Communities like Stack Overflow or dedicated C++ forums can be invaluable when you're stuck.

Keep a Log: Document common errors and their solutions for future reference.

By embracing these troubleshooting strategies, you'll build the resilience and analytical skills needed to tackle even the most stubborn bugs.

7: Conclusion & Next Steps

Congratulations on completing the first chapter of your journey into C++ programming! In this chapter, we introduced you to the power of C++, explained why it remains a cornerstone in software development, and guided you through setting up your development environment. We also explored core concepts, tackled hands-on projects, examined advanced techniques, and addressed common pitfalls.

7.1 Recap of What You've Learned

Let's briefly summarize the key points covered in this chapter:

Why C++?

We discussed the enduring relevance of C++—its performance, flexibility, and control—and why it's a wise investment of your time.

Core Concepts:

You learned about the nature of compiled languages, the benefits of static typing, the importance of memory management, and the foundations of object-oriented programming.

Setting Up Your Environment:

Detailed instructions on choosing an IDE, installing a compiler, and configuring your system were provided to ensure a smooth start.

Hands-On Projects:

Through projects like "Hello, World!", a simple calculator, and an environment verification tool, you put theory into practice.

Advanced Techniques and Troubleshooting:

We introduced you to optimization strategies, advanced debugging techniques, and practical troubleshooting tips that will serve you well as you advance.

7.2 Next Steps in Your Learning Journey

Now that you have a solid foundation, here are some recommended next steps:

Practice Regularly:

The best way to internalize what you've learned is to write code every day. Tinker with the examples provided and try to modify them to see how changes affect the output.

Explore More Projects:

Challenge yourself with new projects. Perhaps develop a simple game, a data processing tool, or an interactive command-line application.

Deepen Your Understanding:

As you become more comfortable with the basics, delve deeper into advanced topics like object-oriented design patterns, memory optimization techniques, and template programming.

Engage with the Community:

Join online forums, attend local coding meetups, and contribute to open-source projects. Sharing your experiences and learning from others can accelerate your progress.

7.3 Additional Resources

To further support your learning, here are some resources you may find helpful:

Books:

"The C++ Programming Language" by Bjarne Stroustrup

"Effective Modern C++" by Scott Meyers

Websites and Tutorials:

cppreference.com – an excellent reference for C++ syntax and libraries

LearnCPP.com – a free tutorial for C++ programming

Communities:

Stack Overflow – for troubleshooting and code review

Reddit's r/cpp – for community discussions and advice

7.4 Final Words of Encouragement

Learning C++ is both challenging and rewarding. As you continue your journey, remember that every expert was once a beginner. Embrace the challenges, celebrate your progress, and don't be discouraged by setbacks. The skills you develop here will serve as a strong foundation for a successful career in software development.

Keep this chapter as a reference, and revisit the troubleshooting tips and best practices whenever you feel stuck. With persistence, curiosity, and a willingness to learn, you'll soon be building sophisticated, efficient, and robust software applications in C++.

CHAPTER 2: GETTING STARTED WITH C++

1; Introduction

Welcome to Chapter 2: Getting Started with C++. In this chapter, we embark on an exciting journey into the world of C++—a language renowned for its performance, efficiency, and versatility. Whether you're completely new to programming or coming from another language, understanding C++'s roots, its evolution over time, and the fundamentals of writing and building a simple program will empower you to harness its full potential.

Why This Chapter Matters

Before diving into code, it's important to appreciate the context of C++ in today's software landscape. C++ is not only the foundation for many modern programming techniques but also a language that powers critical systems in industries ranging from gaming and finance to aerospace and embedded systems. By understanding its history and the reasons behind its design decisions, you can develop a deeper appreciation for the language's strengths—and its occasional challenges.

Key Concepts and Terminology

In this chapter, you will learn about:

History & Evolution of C++: Discover how C++ emerged from the C language, its progression through various standards (C++98, C++11, C++14, C++17, C++20, and beyond), and its impact on modern software development.

Writing Your First "Hello, World!" Program: Experience the thrill of creating a simple program that introduces you to C++ syntax, compilation, and execution.

Understanding the Build Process: Learn how your C++ code is transformed from human-readable source files into a machine-executable program, and why this process is so crucial for performance and reliability.

As you read through this chapter, keep in mind that each concept is carefully chosen to build a strong foundation. We'll begin with the fascinating history of the language, move through practical coding examples, and conclude with insights into advanced build techniques and troubleshooting.

The tone throughout this chapter is professional yet approachable. Our aim is to make complex ideas accessible, using clear explanations, analogies, and practical examples. Whether you're planning to write software for fun or aiming to develop professional-grade applications, this chapter sets the stage for a rewarding learning experience.

By the end of this chapter, you will have not only written your first C++ program but also developed an understanding of how that program is built and executed on your computer. This is an essential stepping stone towards mastering more advanced topics in later chapters. Let's get started!

2: Core Concepts and Theory

In this section, we delve into the core concepts behind C++—from its storied past to the principles that govern its design. A solid grasp of these fundamentals will help you understand not just the "how" but also the "why" behind the code you write.

2.1 The History & Evolution of C++

C++ was created by Bjarne Stroustrup in the early 1980s as an enhancement to the C programming language. Originally called "C with Classes," it was designed to incorporate object-oriented features while maintaining C's efficiency. Let's explore the major milestones:

The Birth of C++ (Early 1980s):

Initially developed at Bell Labs, C++ aimed to extend C's procedural capabilities with object-oriented features like classes, inheritance, and polymorphism. This allowed developers to write more modular, reusable code.

Standardization (C++98 and C++03):

The first international standard for C++ was published in 1998, followed by a minor revision in 2003. These standards established a solid base, including the Standard Template Library (STL), which provided generic data structures and algorithms.

Modern C++ (C++11 Onwards):

C++11 introduced major enhancements such as auto type deduction, lambda expressions, and smart pointers. Subsequent standards (C++14, C++17, C++20) continued to add features that simplify coding, improve safety, and boost performance.

Analogy:
Imagine the evolution of C++ as a car that has been continuously upgraded over decades. The original model was robust and efficient, but modern iterations come with enhanced safety features, better fuel efficiency, and smarter controls—making the ride smoother and more enjoyable.

2.2 Why the History Matters

Understanding the evolution of C++ gives you insight into its design philosophies. Many of its advanced features are direct responses to the challenges faced by early programmers:

Efficiency: Early systems demanded high performance, so C++ was built with low-level memory manipulation in mind.

Modularity: As software systems grew in complexity, the need for reusable components led to the adoption of object-oriented principles.

Flexibility: C++ supports multiple programming paradigms, allowing you to choose the best approach for a given problem.

By knowing where C++ came from, you can better appreciate its strengths and limitations. This historical context informs best practices and guides you in writing robust, efficient code.

2.3 Fundamental Theories Behind C++ Programming

Beyond history, several core theories underpin the language:

Compiled Language Paradigm:

C++ is a compiled language, meaning your code is translated into machine code before execution. This results in high performance but also requires careful management of compilation and linking processes.

Static Typing:

Every variable in C++ has a defined type at compile time, which helps catch errors early and allows for optimizations.

Object-Oriented Principles:

Encapsulation, inheritance, and polymorphism are central. These principles help organize code into manageable, reusable pieces.

Memory Management:

Unlike many modern languages that handle memory automatically, C++ gives you direct control over allocation and deallocation. This control is powerful but requires discipline to avoid memory leaks and other issues.

2.4 The Role of the Build Process

Before you can run your C++ code, it must go through the build process:

Preprocessing:
The preprocessor handles directives like #include and #define, preparing the source code for compilation.

Compilation:
The compiler translates the preprocessed code into assembly language.

Assembly:
An assembler converts the assembly code into machine code.

Linking:
The linker combines various pieces of code (and libraries) into a single executable.

Understanding each of these steps is vital. It helps you diagnose errors, optimize your code, and appreciate the performance advantages that compiled languages offer.

2.5 Bringing It All Together

Let's consider a simple example to illustrate these core concepts. Imagine you're writing a program that prints "Hello, World!" on the screen. Even this simple task involves several layers of theory:

Historical Significance:

"Hello, World!" is the traditional first program in many languages, symbolizing the start of one's journey.

Static Typing & Memory Management:

Even a simple program declares variables and uses functions, reinforcing these concepts.

Build Process:

The program must be preprocessed, compiled, assembled, and linked before you see the output.

In the next section, we'll provide a step-by-step guide on setting up the tools needed to write and build C++ programs.

3: Tools and Setup

Before you can write your first C++ program, it's essential to set up your development environment. This section will guide you through choosing the right tools, installing a compiler, and configuring your system so you can focus on learning C++ without technical roadblocks.

3.1 Choosing an IDE or Text Editor

An Integrated Development Environment (IDE) can simplify coding with features like syntax highlighting, code completion, and debugging tools. Here are some popular options:

Visual Studio (Windows):

A powerful IDE with comprehensive debugging and project management features.

CLion (Cross-Platform):

JetBrains' IDE offers robust support for C++ with smart code analysis and refactoring tools.

Code::Blocks (Cross-Platform):

A free, open-source IDE that's lightweight and customizable.

Visual Studio Code (VS Code):

With the right extensions, VS Code becomes a flexible editor for C++ development.

Tip: For beginners, a user-friendly IDE like Code::Blocks or Visual Studio can help reduce the learning curve.

3.2 Installing a Compiler

C++ code must be compiled into an executable, so installing a compiler is a critical step. Here's how to set up compilers on different platforms:

Windows – Installing MinGW (GCC)

Download MinGW:

Visit the MinGW website and download the installer.

Install MinGW:

Follow the installation wizard and choose the appropriate options.

Set Environment Variables:

Add the MinGW bin directory to your PATH. For example, open Command Prompt and run:

```shell
set PATH=%PATH%;C:\MinGW\bin
```

Verify Installation:

Run:

```shell
g++ --version
```

to confirm that GCC is installed.

macOS – Installing Xcode Command Line Tools

Open Terminal:

Launch Terminal from Applications > Utilities.

Install Tools:

Run:

```shell
xcode-select --install
```

Verify Installation:

Check the installation by running:

```shell
gcc --version
```

Linux – Installing GCC

For most distributions, GCC is available via the package manager. For example, on Ubuntu:

```shell
sudo apt update
sudo apt install build-essential
```

3.3 Configuring Your Development Environment

Once you have your IDE and compiler installed, consider these configuration steps:

Project Organization:

Create a dedicated folder for your C++ projects. For example:

css

```
CppProjects/
├── HelloWorld/
│     └── main.cpp
└── SimpleCalculator/
      └── main.cpp
```

Editor Preferences:

Customize themes, font sizes, and indentation settings to enhance readability and comfort.

Version Control:

Use Git for version control. Install Git and consider setting up a GitHub repository for your projects. This practice helps track changes and manage revisions.

3.4 Verifying Your Setup

To ensure everything is working correctly, create a simple "Hello, World!" program (which we'll explore in the next section) and compile it. This verification confirms that your IDE, compiler, and environment variables are correctly configured.

4: Hands-on Examples & Projects

Now that we've covered the theory and set up your tools, it's time for hands-on practice. In this section, you'll build your first C++ program, understand each step of the build process, and see how theory translates into real-world coding. We'll walk through several projects, starting with the classic "Hello, World!" program and then exploring variations that reinforce core concepts.

4.1 Project 1: Your First "Hello, World!" Program

4.1.1 Overview

The "Hello, World!" program is a time-honored tradition in programming. Its simplicity allows you to focus on the process of writing, compiling, and running code without getting overwhelmed by complexity.

4.1.2 Step-by-Step Walkthrough

Create the Source File:

Open your IDE and create a new file named main.cpp in your project folder.

Write the Code:

Type the following code:

```cpp
// main.cpp: A simple program to print "Hello, World!"
#include <iostream> // Include the standard input/output stream library


int main() (
    std::cout << "Hello, World!" << std::endl;  // Output message to the console
    return 0;  // Indicate that the program ended successfully
)
```

Explanation:

The #include <iostream> directive imports the library needed for input and output.

The main() function is the entry point of the program.

std::cout outputs text to the console, and std::endl adds a new line.

Compile the Program:

If you are using an IDE, click the "Build" or "Compile" button. Alternatively, from the command line, run:

```shell
g++ main.cpp -o HelloWorld
```

This command tells the compiler to generate an executable named HelloWorld.

Run the Executable:

In your IDE or via the command line:

```shell
./HelloWorld
```

You should see:

Hello, World!

4.1.3 Variations and Experiments

Once you've successfully run your program, try these experiments:

Change the Output:

Modify the text within the quotes to personalize your greeting.

Add Comments:

Experiment with adding more comments to explain each line of code.

Explore Formatting:

Use escape sequences like \n to add new lines or \t for tabs.

4.2 Project 2: Exploring the Build Process

Understanding the build process is crucial. In this project, you will manually run each step of the process to see how your source code transforms into an executable.

4.2.1 Breaking Down the Build Process

Preprocessing:
The preprocessor handles directives (e.g., #include, #define). You can view the preprocessed output by running:

```shell
g++ -E main.cpp -o preprocessed.txt
```

Open preprocessed.txt to see how the code is expanded.

Compilation:
The compiler converts your preprocessed code into assembly code. Generate the assembly code using:

shell

g++ -S main.cpp -o main.s

Examine main.s to see the assembly instructions generated from your source code.

Assembly:
The assembler then converts the assembly code into machine code (object files). This step is usually integrated into the compilation process.

Linking:
Finally, the linker combines object files and libraries into the final executable.

Tip: Use the -v flag during compilation to see verbose output that details each of these steps.

4.2.2 Hands-on Walkthrough

Let's walk through these steps with our "Hello, World!" program:

Step 1: Preprocess

shell

g++ -E main.cpp -o preprocessed.txt

Open and review the file to see how header files and macros are expanded.

Step 2: Compile to Assembly

shell

g++ -S main.cpp -o main.s

Inspect main.s to gain insight into the low-level instructions.

Step 3: Build the Executable

shell

g++ main.cpp -o HelloWorld

Run the executable to confirm the process works.

4.2.3 What You Learn

This project reinforces several key ideas:

The layered nature of the build process.

How each stage transforms your code.

The importance of compiler flags and options in controlling the build.

4.3 Project 3: Extending "Hello, World!" with User Input

Now that you understand the basics, let's extend your program to interact with the user. This project introduces variables, basic I/O, and error checking.

4.3.1 Project Overview

In this project, your program will:

Ask for the user's name.

Greet the user by name.

Demonstrate simple input handling and string manipulation.

4.3.2 Writing the Code

Create a new file named greeting.cpp and add the following code:

```cpp
// greeting.cpp: A program that greets the user by name
#include <iostream>
#include <string>

int main() {
    std::string name;
    std::cout << "Enter your name: ";
    std::getline(std::cin, name);  // Read an entire line of input
    std::cout << "Hello, " << name << "!" << std::endl;
```

```
    return 0;
)
```

Explanation:

We include the <string> library to work with C++ strings.

std::getline allows us to capture the full input line, including spaces.

4.3.3 Compiling and Running

Compile the program:

```shell
g++ greeting.cpp -o Greeting
```
Run the executable:

```shell
./Greeting
```
When prompted, enter your name. The program should greet you accordingly.

4.4 Integrating the Build Process into Your Workflow

At this stage, you should start incorporating build process insights into your regular workflow:

Automating Builds:

Learn to write simple Makefiles to automate compiling multiple files.

Using IDE Build Tools:

Explore how your IDE manages build steps and customize these settings as needed.

Example: A Simple Makefile

Create a file named Makefile in your project directory:

```makefile
# Makefile for HelloWorld project
```

```
CC = g++
CFLAGS = -Wall -O2

all: HelloWorld

HelloWorld: main.cpp
        $(CC) $(CFLAGS) main.cpp -o HelloWorld
```

clean:

> **rm -f HelloWorld**

Explanation:

CC defines the compiler.

CFLAGS includes flags for warnings and optimization.

The all target builds the executable, while clean removes it.

4.5 Real-World Applications

Even simple projects like these build a foundation for more complex applications. For example:

Interactive Applications:

Using basic I/O and build automation, you can create command-line tools.

Learning Debugging:

By dissecting the build process, you'll be better prepared to troubleshoot errors as your projects grow in complexity.

Throughout these projects, always aim to write clean, well-commented code. Regularly test and iterate on your projects to build confidence in your abilities.

5: Advanced Techniques & Optimization

Even at the beginner stage, it's valuable to touch on techniques that will help you write more efficient code and optimize the build process.

5.1 Compiler Optimization Flags

Modern compilers offer various flags to optimize code. For example:

-O2 and -O3:

Enable optimization levels that improve runtime performance.

-g:
Includes debugging information without optimization interference.

Example:

```shell
g++ -O2 -g main.cpp -o HelloWorldOptimized
```

This command balances performance improvements with the ability to debug.

5.2 Modularization and Code Organization

As your projects grow, breaking your code into modules (separate files for declarations and implementations) becomes essential. This improves maintainability and speeds up the build process.

Example: Splitting Code into Header and Source Files

Create a header file greetings.h:

```cpp
// greetings.h: Function declaration for greeting
functionality
#ifndef GREETINGS_H
#define GREETINGS_H

#include <string>
```

```cpp
void greetUser(const std::string &name);
```

```cpp
#endif // GREETINGS_H
```

And the implementation in greetings.cpp:

```cpp
cpp
// greetings.cpp: Function implementation
#include "greetings.h"
#include <iostream>

void greetUser(const std::string &name) {
    std::cout << "Hello, " << name << "!" << std::endl;
}
```

Now, modify your main.cpp:

```cpp
cpp
// main.cpp: Uses the greetUser function
#include "greetings.h"
#include <iostream>

int main() {
    std::string name;
    std::cout << "Enter your name: ";
    std::getline(std::cin, name);
    greetUser(name);
    return 0;
}
```

Explanation:
Modularization helps isolate functionality and makes code reuse easier.

5.3 Advanced Build System Concepts

Beyond simple Makefiles, you can explore build systems like CMake for managing larger projects. CMake simplifies the process of generating platform-specific build files and handling dependencies.

Example: Basic CMakeLists.txt

```cmake
cmake
cmake_minimum_required(VERSION 3.10)
project(HelloWorld)

set(CMAKE_CXX_STANDARD 11)

add_executable(HelloWorld main.cpp greetings.cpp)
```

Using CMake, you can configure, build, and maintain multi-platform projects with ease.

5.4 Performance Profiling

Once your programs start to get more complex, you might need to profile your code to find bottlenecks. Tools like gprof or integrated IDE profilers can help you identify inefficient code paths.

5.5 Best Practices for Optimized Builds

Minimize Recompilation:

Structure your code to limit the files that need recompiling when changes are made.

Use Precompiled Headers:

They speed up the compilation process by caching frequently used headers.

Leverage Incremental Builds:

Use tools that only rebuild modified parts of your project.

By incorporating these advanced techniques early, you set the stage for efficient, scalable projects as you progress in your C++ journey.

6: Troubleshooting and Problem-Solving

No learning process is without obstacles. In this section, we address common challenges you might face as you write, compile, and run your C++ programs—and offer strategies to overcome them.

6.1 Common Compilation Errors

6.1.1 Syntax Errors

Errors like missing semicolons or mismatched braces are common when you're just starting. Always read the error messages carefully:

Example Error:

go

error: expected ';' before ')' token

Solution:
Review the line indicated and ensure every statement ends with a semicolon.

6.1.2 Include and Namespace Issues

If you see errors such as "'cout' was not declared in this scope," ensure you:

Include the correct header (#include <iostream>).

Use the proper namespace (either prefix with std:: or include using namespace std;).

6.2 Troubleshooting the Build Process

Issues during preprocessing, compilation, or linking can be daunting:

Preprocessing Errors:

Verify that all header files exist and that include paths are correctly specified.

Linking Errors:

Missing function definitions often indicate that some source files were not compiled or linked.

Debugging Tips:

Verbose Mode:

Use flags like -v to see detailed output during compilation.

Step-by-Step Build:

Manually run the preprocessing (-E), assembly (-S), and linking steps to isolate where the error occurs.

6.3 Debugging Tools

Familiarize yourself with debugging tools such as GDB:

Starting GDB:

```shell
g++ -g main.cpp -o DebugHelloWorld
gdb DebugHelloWorld
```

Common Commands:

break main to set a breakpoint at the start of main().

run to start execution.

step and next to navigate through code.

6.4 Developing a Problem-Solving Mindset

Effective troubleshooting requires a systematic approach:

Isolate the Problem:

Comment out sections of code to narrow down the source of the error.

Search Online:

Platforms like Stack Overflow and C++ forums are invaluable resources.

Document Your Findings:

Keep a log of common issues and solutions for future reference.

By applying these problem-solving techniques, you'll not only fix errors faster but also develop skills that will help you in larger, more complex projects.

7: Conclusion & Next Steps

Congratulations on completing this deep dive into getting started with C++. In this chapter, you've learned about the fascinating history and evolution of the language, written your very first "Hello, World!" program, and gained an understanding of the build process that transforms your code into an executable.

7.1 Recap of Key Points

History & Evolution:

You discovered how C++ evolved from "C with Classes" into the robust, multi-paradigm language it is today. Understanding this history helps illuminate many design choices in modern C++.

Your First Program:

Writing "Hello, World!" provided you with a hands-on introduction to the language's syntax and structure.

Build Process:

By dissecting the build process—from preprocessing to linking—you've gained insights into how your code is transformed and optimized.

7.2 Next Steps in Your C++ Journey

Now that you have a solid foundation, consider these next steps:

Practice:
Keep writing small programs to reinforce the concepts learned. Experiment with modifying your "Hello, World!" program or creating new variations.

Explore Further:

Delve into topics such as control structures, functions, and data structures in upcoming chapters.

Engage with the Community:

Join forums, attend meetups, and contribute to open-source projects to learn from experienced developers.

7.3 Additional Resources

To continue your learning, here are some resources:

Books:

"The C++ Programming Language" by Bjarne Stroustrup

"Effective Modern C++" by Scott Meyers

Websites:

cppreference.com for detailed documentation

LearnCPP.com for structured tutorials

Communities:

Stack Overflow, Reddit's r/cpp, and local coding meetups

7.4 Final Words

Learning C++ is a journey filled with both challenges and rewards. Every line of code you write brings you closer to mastering a language that powers some of the world's most critical software systems. Take pride in your progress, remain curious, and remember that persistence is key. As you move forward, the tools, techniques, and insights gained in this chapter will serve as a strong foundation for your continued growth in C++ programming.

CHAPTER 3: CONTROL STRUCTURES AND FUNCTIONS

1; Introduction

Welcome to Chapter 3: Control Structures and Functions. In any programming language, the ability to control the flow of your code and to modularize tasks into reusable blocks is paramount. In C++, control structures—such as conditionals and loops—allow you to dictate the logic behind your programs, while functions help you break down complex tasks into manageable pieces. Mastering these concepts is essential for writing efficient, readable, and maintainable code.

Why Control Structures and Functions Matter

Control structures are the backbone of decision-making in your programs. They allow your code to react to different conditions and execute specific blocks of code based on user input or program state. Functions, on the other hand, are the building blocks that let you encapsulate repetitive tasks and improve code reusability. Together, these constructs empower you to create dynamic, interactive, and sophisticated applications.

Imagine building a temperature converter—a simple yet effective project that uses conditionals to handle user choices (e.g., Celsius to Fahrenheit versus Fahrenheit to Celsius) and loops to allow multiple conversions until the user decides to exit. This real-world application is not only a practical exercise but also a window into how complex software systems can be built from small, understandable parts.

Key Concepts and Terminology

Throughout this chapter, you'll encounter several key concepts:

Conditionals: These are the "if-else" statements and "switch" cases that let your program decide what to do based on certain conditions.

Loops: Repetitive structures such as "for," "while," and "do-while" loops enable your code to execute a block multiple times.

Functions: Blocks of code that perform specific tasks and can be called from various parts of your program.

Modularity: The idea of breaking your program into smaller, reusable pieces, making it easier to maintain and debug.

Setting the Tone for the Journey Ahead

This chapter is crafted in a professional, yet approachable tone. We will begin by exploring the theoretical underpinnings of control structures and functions, using real-world analogies to simplify complex ideas. Next, we'll guide you through setting up your development environment and provide a step-by-step walkthrough of writing code. Finally, you'll complete the chapter with a hands-on project—a Temperature Converter—that ties together all the concepts learned.

By the end of this chapter, you will be comfortable with writing conditional statements, implementing loops, and creating functions in C++. You will also have developed a practical project that demonstrates how these elements come together to solve real-world problems. Let's dive in and start transforming your ideas into efficient, well-organized code!

2: Core Concepts and Theory

In this section, we explore the core concepts behind control structures and functions. We will detail how conditionals and loops control the flow of execution and how functions encapsulate behavior. Understanding these concepts will provide the theoretical foundation you need to write robust and modular C++ programs.

2.1 Understanding Conditionals

Conditionals allow your program to make decisions. The simplest form of a conditional statement in C++ is the if statement. Consider the following example:

```cpp
#include <iostream>

int main() {
    int temperature = 25;
    if (temperature > 30) {
        std::cout << "It's a hot day." << std::endl;
    } else {
        std::cout << "It's not too hot today." << std::endl;
    }
    return 0;
}
```

Explanation:

The program checks if the temperature is greater than 30.

If the condition is true, it prints a message indicating that it is hot; otherwise, it prints a different message.

Real-World Analogy:

Imagine you're deciding whether to carry an umbrella. You check the weather forecast (the condition) and then decide based on whether it's raining or not.

Variations of Conditionals

If-Else Statements:

Allows for two possible outcomes.

Else-If Chains:

Multiple conditions can be checked sequentially.

Switch Statements:

Useful when you need to choose between multiple discrete options.

```cpp
#include <iostream>

int main() {
    char unit;
    std::cout << "Enter temperature unit (C/F): ";
    std::cin >> unit;

    switch(unit) {
        case 'C':
        case 'c':
            std::cout << "Converting from Celsius." << std::endl;
            break;
        case 'F':
        case 'f':
            std::cout << "Converting from Fahrenheit." << std::endl;
            break;
        default:
            std::cout << "Invalid unit!" << std::endl;
    }
    return 0;
}
```

2.2 The Role of Loops

Loops are essential when you want your program to perform repetitive tasks. C++ provides several types of loops:

For Loops

Ideal for situations where the number of iterations is known:

```cpp
```

```cpp
#include <iostream>

int main() {
    for (int i = 0; i < 5; i++) {
        std::cout << "Iteration " << i + 1 << std::endl;
    }
    return 0;
}
```
Explanation:

The loop runs five times, printing a message each time.

While Loops

Best used when the number of iterations isn't predetermined:

```cpp
cpp
#include <iostream>

int main() {
    int count = 0;
    while (count < 5) {
        std::cout << "Count is " << count << std::endl;
        count++;
    }
    return 0;
}
```
Do-While Loops

Guarantees that the loop executes at least once:

```cpp
cpp
#include <iostream>

int main() {
    int count = 0;
    do {
```

```cpp
        std::cout << "Do-while loop iteration " << count + 1 <<
std::endl;
        count++;
    ) while (count < 5);
    return 0;
)
```

Analogy:
Think of loops as the repetitive actions you perform every morning—brushing your teeth, making coffee, and so on—until a certain condition (like leaving for work) is met.

2.3 Functions: Encapsulating Behavior

Functions are self-contained blocks of code that perform a specific task. They promote reusability and modularity. Here's an example of a simple function that calculates the square of a number:

```cpp
cpp
#include <iostream>

// Function declaration
int square(int num);

int main() (
    int number = 5;
    std::cout << "The square of " << number << " is " <<
square(number) << std::endl;
    return 0;
)

// Function definition
int square(int num) (
    return num * num;
)
```

Key Points:

Declaration: Tells the compiler about the function's name, return type, and parameters.

Definition: Contains the actual code that executes when the function is called.

Return Statement: Sends the computed value back to the caller.

Advantages of Using Functions:

Reusability: Write once, use multiple times.

Modularity: Divide your program into logical blocks.

Maintainability: Changes in a function affect all calls to it, reducing redundancy.

2.4 Scope and Lifetime

Understanding variable scope (where a variable is accessible) and lifetime (how long it exists) is crucial when using functions and loops. Variables declared inside a function are local to that function and cannot be accessed outside. Global variables, although accessible everywhere, should be used sparingly to avoid conflicts.

2.5 Combining Control Structures and Functions

When you combine conditionals, loops, and functions, you can build complex programs in an organized manner. For example, a function can process user input using a loop and then return a result based on conditional checks. This separation of concerns makes your code easier to read, test, and maintain.

By mastering these core concepts, you'll be ready to apply them in practical scenarios. In the next section, we'll set up the tools necessary to write and test your C++ programs effectively.

3: Tools and Setup

Before diving into coding, it is essential to set up a robust development environment. In this section, we'll cover the necessary tools, IDEs, and compilers to ensure you have everything required for writing, compiling, and running your C++ code.

3.1 Choosing Your Development Environment

For beginners, a well-integrated environment makes learning much smoother. Consider these popular IDEs and text editors:

Visual Studio Code (VS Code):

Lightweight, cross-platform, and with numerous extensions for C++.

Code::Blocks:
A free, open-source IDE tailored for C++.

CLion:
A feature-rich, cross-platform IDE from JetBrains (requires a license for full features).

Visual Studio (Windows):

Comprehensive tools and debuggers for Windows development.

Tip: If you're just starting, VS Code or Code::Blocks is a great choice due to their ease of use and wide community support.

3.2 Installing a Compiler

C++ is a compiled language, so you'll need a compiler to translate your code into an executable. Here's how to install a compiler on various platforms:

Windows: Installing MinGW (GCC)

Download and Install:

Visit the MinGW website and follow the installer instructions.

Set Environment Variables:

Add the path to the MinGW bin directory to your system's PATH variable.

shell

```
set PATH=%PATH%;C:\MinGW\bin
```
Verify Installation:

Open Command Prompt and run:

```
shell
g++ --version
```
macOS: Installing Xcode Command Line Tools

Open Terminal:

Launch Terminal from Applications > Utilities.

Install Tools:

Execute:

```
shell
xcode-select --install
```
Verify Installation:

Run:

```
shell
gcc --version
```
Linux: Installing GCC

For Ubuntu or Debian-based distributions, use:

```
shell
sudo apt update
sudo apt install build-essential
```

3.3 Configuring Your IDE

After installing your compiler, configure your IDE:

Project Structure:

Organize your projects into dedicated folders. For example:

css

```
CppProjects/
├── TemperatureConverter/
│   ├── main.cpp
│   ├── converter.h
│   └── converter.cpp
```

Editor Settings:

Set your preferences for code formatting, themes, and auto-completion.

Version Control:

Install Git and, if possible, link your projects to an online repository like GitHub. This practice helps in version tracking and collaboration.

3.4 Testing Your Environment

Before moving to more complex examples, create a simple "Hello, World!" program (if not already done in Chapter 2) to verify your setup:

```cpp
cpp
#include <iostream>
int main() (
    std::cout << "Hello, World!" << std::endl;
    return 0;
)
```

Compile and run your program. This confirms that your IDE, compiler, and environment variables are all correctly configured.

4: Hands-on Examples & Projects

Now it's time to put theory into practice. In this section, we'll walk through several practical examples that demonstrate control structures and functions. Our hands-on project—a Temperature Converter—will combine everything you've learned so far.

4.1 Project 1: Building a Temperature Converter

4.1.1 Project Overview

In this project, we will create a console-based Temperature Converter that allows users to convert temperatures between Celsius and Fahrenheit. This project will incorporate:

Conditionals: To determine the conversion direction.

Loops: To allow repeated conversions until the user decides to exit.

Functions: To encapsulate conversion logic and improve code readability.

4.1.2 Step-by-Step Walkthrough

Step 1: Creating the Project Files

Organize your project with the following files:

main.cpp: Contains the main function and user interaction.

converter.h: Contains function declarations.

converter.cpp: Contains function definitions for conversion.

Step 2: Writing the Header File (converter.h)

```cpp
// converter.h: Function declarations for temperature
conversion
#ifndef CONVERTER_H
#define CONVERTER_H

// Converts Celsius to Fahrenheit
double celsiusToFahrenheit(double celsius);

// Converts Fahrenheit to Celsius
double fahrenheitToCelsius(double fahrenheit);
```

```cpp
#endif // CONVERTER_H
```

Step 3: Writing the Function Definitions (converter.cpp)

```cpp
cpp
// converter.cpp: Function definitions for temperature
conversion
#include "converter.h"

// Function to convert Celsius to Fahrenheit
double celsiusToFahrenheit(double celsius) {
    return (celsius * 9.0 / 5.0) + 32;
}

// Function to convert Fahrenheit to Celsius
double fahrenheitToCelsius(double fahrenheit) {
    return (fahrenheit - 32) * 5.0 / 9.0;
}
```

Step 4: Creating the Main Program (main.cpp)

```cpp
cpp
// main.cpp: Temperature Converter program
#include <iostream>
#include "converter.h"

using namespace std;

int main() {
    char choice;
    double temperature, convertedTemp;
    do {
        // Display menu
        cout << "Temperature Converter" << endl;
        cout << "----------------------" << endl;
        cout << "Choose an option:" << endl;
        cout << "1. Convert Celsius to Fahrenheit" << endl;
```

```
cout << "2. Convert Fahrenheit to Celsius" << endl;
cout << "Q. Quit" << endl;
cout << "Enter your choice: ";
cin >> choice;

// Process user choice
if (choice == '1') {
    cout << "Enter temperature in Celsius: ";
    cin >> temperature;
    convertedTemp = celsiusToFahrenheit(temperature);
    cout << temperature << "°C is " << convertedTemp <<
"°F" << endl;
} else if (choice == '2') {
    cout << "Enter temperature in Fahrenheit: ";
    cin >> temperature;
    convertedTemp = fahrenheitToCelsius(temperature);
    cout << temperature << "°F is " << convertedTemp <<
"°C" << endl;
} else if (choice == 'Q' || choice == 'q') {
    cout << "Exiting the converter. Goodbye!" << endl;
} else {
    cout << "Invalid option. Please try again." << endl;
}

cout << endl; // Blank line for readability
} while (choice != 'Q' && choice != 'q');

return 0;
}
```

Explanation:

Menu and Loop: The do-while loop ensures the program repeats until the user decides to quit.

Conditionals: The if-else statements determine which conversion function to call.

Function Calls: The conversion functions (celsiusToFahrenheit and fahrenheitToCelsius) are used to perform the actual calculations.

4.1.3 Compiling and Running the Project

Compile the Code:

Use a Makefile or compile manually:

shell

```
g++ -o TemperatureConverter main.cpp converter.cpp
```

Run the Executable:

shell

```
./TemperatureConverter
```

Test:
Input various temperatures and verify the correct output.

4.2 Additional Examples: Enhancing the Temperature Converter

To further solidify your understanding, consider extending the project:

Input Validation:

Add checks to ensure that the temperature input is numeric.

Multiple Conversions:

Allow the user to convert a batch of temperatures from a file.

User Interface Enhancements:

Use color-coded text or a graphical interface (if you venture into libraries like Qt).

4.3 Code Walkthrough and Best Practices

As you develop projects, follow these guidelines:

Comment Your Code:

Clear comments explain the purpose of each function and control structure.

Modular Design:

Keep your functions small and focused on a single task.

Consistent Formatting:

Use consistent indentation and naming conventions to improve readability.

Before-and-After Example:

Before:
A monolithic block of code mixing user input, processing, and output.

After:
Separated into functions, each handling a specific responsibility (as seen in our Temperature Converter project).

4.4 Exploring Loop Variants in Projects

Experiment with different loops:

Replace the do-while loop with a while loop by initializing the condition before entering the loop.

Implement nested loops for more complex input scenarios (e.g., converting multiple temperature readings in a table).

By working through these examples, you not only reinforce your understanding of control structures and functions but also see firsthand how they form the building blocks of more complex applications.

5: Advanced Techniques & Optimization

Once you've mastered the basics, it's time to explore advanced techniques and optimization strategies that can enhance your code's performance and maintainability.

5.1 Advanced Conditional Structures

Ternary Operator:

A concise alternative to if-else:

```cpp
int result = (a > b) ? a : b;
```

Nested Conditionals:

Use sparingly to handle multi-level decision-making while keeping readability.

5.2 Optimizing Loops

Loop Unrolling:

Manually expand the loop body to reduce overhead (in performance-critical code).

Iterator Optimization:

When working with containers, use iterators to efficiently traverse elements.

5.3 Function Optimization

Inlining Functions:

For small, frequently called functions, use the inline keyword to suggest that the compiler replace the function call with the function code:

```cpp
```

```
inline double square(double num) {
    return num * num;
}
```

Recursion vs. Iteration:

Understand when recursion is appropriate, and optimize recursive functions with techniques like tail recursion.

5.4 Memory and Resource Management

Even simple functions can benefit from:

Avoiding Unnecessary Copies:

Pass variables by reference where appropriate.

Using Const Correctness:

Mark parameters as const when they should not be modified.

5.5 Best Practices for Code Maintenance

Modularization:
Keep functions small and focused.

Documentation:
Use clear comments and maintain updated documentation for each module.

Profiling Tools:

Learn to use tools such as gprof or Valgrind to identify performance bottlenecks.

By incorporating these advanced techniques, you lay the groundwork for writing code that is not only functional but also optimized for performance and long-term maintainability.

6: Troubleshooting and Problem-Solving

Even well-written code can run into issues. This section covers common challenges you might encounter when working with control structures and functions, and offers troubleshooting strategies.

6.1 Common Errors and Their Solutions

6.1.1 Syntax and Logical Errors

Missing Braces or Semicolons:

Ensure every block and statement is properly closed.

Infinite Loops:

Verify loop conditions carefully to avoid infinite iterations.

6.1.2 Function Declaration and Definition Mismatches

Ensure that function declarations in header files match the definitions in source files, including return types and parameter lists.

Before-and-After Example:

Before:
A mismatch causing linker errors.

After:
Correctly matching function prototypes.

6.2 Debugging Techniques

Print Debugging:

Insert print statements to check variable values at critical points.

Using a Debugger:

Tools like GDB allow you to set breakpoints and step through your code.

Verbose Compilation:

Use compiler flags such as -Wall to show all warnings.

6.3 Handling User Input and Validation

Improper user input can lead to unexpected behavior:

Validate inputs using conditionals.

Use error messages to guide the user toward providing correct input.

6.4 Developing a Systematic Approach to Problem-Solving

Isolate the Issue:

Comment out sections of code to narrow down where the problem occurs.

Research and Document:

Use online resources (e.g., Stack Overflow) and keep notes of common issues and solutions.

Iterative Testing:

Make one change at a time and test immediately to see its impact.

By applying these troubleshooting methods, you'll build resilience and become more adept at identifying and resolving issues in your programs.

7: Conclusion & Next Steps

Congratulations on completing Chapter 3: Control Structures and Functions! You have learned how to use conditionals and loops to direct your program's flow and how to create functions to modularize your code. By working through the Temperature Converter project, you applied these concepts in a practical, real-world scenario.

7.1 Recap of Key Concepts

Control Structures:

You explored if-else, switch statements, and various loop constructs, learning how to implement decision-making and repetitive execution in your programs.

Functions:
You learned how to declare, define, and call functions, understanding how they promote code reusability and modular design.

Project Integration:

Through the Temperature Converter project, you combined conditionals, loops, and functions to create an interactive, user-friendly application.

7.2   Reflections   and   Practical Applications

Think about how the control structures and functions you learned here apply to other programming challenges. Whether it's processing data, managing user input, or automating repetitive tasks, these concepts are universally applicable in software development.

7.3 Next Steps in Your C++ Journey

Practice and Experiment:

Continue building small projects that incorporate loops, conditionals, and functions. Try modifying the Temperature Converter to handle additional conversion types or to include error-checking mechanisms.

Deepen Your Knowledge:

Explore advanced topics such as recursion, function overloading, and lambda expressions in upcoming chapters.

Engage with the Community:

Participate in coding forums and local meetups to share your projects and learn from others.

7.4 Additional Resources

To further support your learning:

Books:

"C++ Primer" by Stanley B. Lippman et al.

"Effective C++" by Scott Meyers

Websites:

cppreference.com for detailed reference documentation

LearnCPP.com for tutorials and exercises

Online Courses and Tutorials:

Look for interactive courses that offer hands-on coding practice.

7.5 Final Words of Encouragement

The ability to control program flow and encapsulate functionality is a fundamental skill in programming. Remember, every expert was once a beginner. By practicing these concepts and building projects, you're laying a solid foundation for more advanced programming challenges. Keep experimenting, learning, and refining your code. Happy coding, and enjoy the journey ahead in mastering C++!

CHAPTER 4: CONTROL STRUCTURES AND FUNCTIONS

1; Introduction

Welcome to Chapter 4: Control Structures and Functions. In this chapter, we embark on a journey that delves into two of the most critical aspects of programming in C++—control structures and functions. These core elements are the building blocks that allow you to dictate the flow of your program and to encapsulate reusable code segments. Whether you're new to programming or are looking to solidify your understanding, mastering these concepts is essential to writing clean, efficient, and maintainable software.

The Significance of Control Structures and Functions

Imagine writing a set of instructions without any means to make decisions or to repeat tasks—your program would be as lifeless as a script with no flow. Control structures like **if-else statements**, **switch cases**, and various kinds of **loops** enable your code to make decisions, execute certain blocks repeatedly, and adapt based on changing data or user inputs. Meanwhile, functions help you modularize your code, breaking down complex tasks into smaller, manageable, and reusable pieces. They allow you to abstract away details so that your main program remains clear and focused on high-level logic.

For instance, consider a Temperature Converter application: by using control structures, you can prompt the user for input, decide which conversion to apply based on their choice, and then loop through multiple conversions until the user decides to exit. Functions let you separate the conversion logic from the user interface, making your code more readable and easier to maintain.

Key Concepts and Terminology

Throughout this chapter, you will become familiar with several fundamental concepts:

Conditionals: Structures that allow your program to perform different actions based on boolean expressions (e.g., if, else if, else, and switch).

Loops: Mechanisms to repeat a block of code multiple times (e.g., for, while, and do-while loops).

Functions: Self-contained blocks of code designed to perform specific tasks. They improve reusability and modularity.

Modularity: The practice of dividing a program into separate components, each responsible for a specific part of the program's functionality.

Why You Should Care

Mastering control structures and functions is essential because they form the backbone of effective programming. By the end of this chapter, you will:

Understand how to guide the flow of your program using decision-making constructs.

Be able to implement loops that iterate over data efficiently.

Know how to write functions that encapsulate logic and make your code more organized.

Apply these concepts to build a practical, real-world application: a Temperature Converter.

Setting the Tone

Our approach is professional yet approachable. We'll break down complex ideas into manageable parts, use real-world analogies to relate technical concepts to everyday experiences, and include practical examples and code samples. Imagine control structures as the traffic signals that guide vehicles on a busy road and functions as the specialized workshops where specific tasks are performed. With this mindset, you'll find that even the most complex programs become a series of simple, manageable steps.

By the end of this chapter, you will be well-equipped with the skills to control program flow and write modular code. This foundational knowledge will serve you throughout your C++ journey and enable you to tackle more advanced topics with confidence.

2: Core Concepts and Theory

In this section, we dive deep into the theoretical underpinnings of control structures and functions. We will explore the various types of conditionals and loops, discuss their advantages and proper usage, and examine how functions are defined, declared, and invoked. Through detailed explanations and analogies, we aim to demystify these concepts and prepare you for practical application.

2.1 Understanding Conditionals

2.1.1 The Role of Decision Making

At its core, a conditional statement in programming is similar to making a decision in real life. For example, when deciding what to wear based on the weather, you might say, "If it's raining, then I'll take an umbrella; otherwise, I'll wear sunglasses." In C++, conditional statements let you execute specific blocks of code based on whether a given condition evaluates to true or false.

2.1.2 If-Else Statements

The simplest form of conditional is the **if-else** statement. Consider the following code snippet:

```cpp
#include <iostream>
using namespace std;

int main() {
    int temperature = 28;
    if (temperature > 30) {
        cout << "It is a hot day." << endl;
    } else {
        cout << "It is a pleasant day." << endl;
    }
```

```
    return 0;
)
```

Explanation:

The program checks whether the variable temperature is greater than 30.

If the condition is true, the code inside the first block executes; if not, the code inside the else block runs.

2.1.3 Else-If and Nested Conditionals

Often, you might have more than two possible outcomes. The **else-if** chain allows multiple conditions:

```cpp
cpp
#include <iostream>
using namespace std;

int main() (
    int temperature = 18;
    if (temperature > 30) (
        cout << "It is very hot." << endl;
    ) else if (temperature > 20) (
        cout << "It is warm." << endl;
    ) else if (temperature > 10) (
        cout << "It is cool." << endl;
    ) else (
        cout << "It is cold." << endl;
    )
    return 0;
)
```

Real-World Analogy:

Imagine checking a series of conditions to decide what mode of transportation to take based on the weather. Each condition (rain, snow, clear skies) directs you to a different choice.

2.1.4 Switch Statements

The **switch** statement is another way to handle multiple discrete conditions. It's particularly useful when comparing a single variable against many constant values:

```cpp
#include <iostream>
using namespace std;

int main() {
    char unit;
    cout << "Enter temperature unit (C for Celsius, F for Fahrenheit): ";
    cin >> unit;

    switch (unit) {
        case 'C':
        case 'c':
            cout << "You have selected Celsius." << endl;
            break;
        case 'F':
        case 'f':
            cout << "You have selected Fahrenheit." << endl;
            break;
        default:
            cout << "Invalid selection!" << endl;
    }
    return 0;
}
```

Key Points:

The switch statement checks the value of unit against predefined cases.

The break statement prevents fall-through, ensuring that only the matching case is executed.

2.2 Mastering Loops

Loops allow you to execute a block of code repeatedly until a certain condition is met. They are indispensable for tasks such as iterating over arrays or processing user input repeatedly.

2.2.1 For Loops

For loops are ideal when the number of iterations is known beforehand:

```cpp
#include <iostream>
using namespace std;

int main() {
    for (int i = 0; i < 5; i++) {
        cout << "Iteration " << i + 1 << endl;
    }
    return 0;
}
```

Explanation:

The loop variable i is initialized to 0.

The condition i < 5 is checked before each iteration.

The variable i increments after each loop, and the process repeats.

2.2.2 While Loops

While loops are best used when the number of iterations is not predetermined:

```cpp
#include <iostream>
using namespace std;

int main() {
    int count = 0;
    while (count < 5) {
        cout << "Count: " << count << endl;
```

```cpp
        count++;
    )
    return 0;
)
```

Key Consideration:

Ensure that the loop's condition will eventually become false; otherwise, the loop may run indefinitely.

2.2.3 Do-While Loops

A **do-while loop** guarantees that the loop's body is executed at least once, even if the condition is false initially:

```cpp
cpp
#include <iostream>
using namespace std;

int main() (
    int count = 0;
    do (
        cout << "Do-While Loop Iteration: " << count + 1 << endl;
        count++;
    ) while (count < 5);
    return 0;
)
```

Analogy:
Think of a do-while loop as trying a new recipe at least once before deciding whether you like it.

2.3 Functions: The Building Blocks of Modular Code

Functions are a fundamental part of C++ programming. They help you organize code into reusable blocks, making your programs easier to understand and maintain.

2.3.1 Function Declaration and Definition

Consider a simple function that computes the square of a number:

```cpp
#include <iostream>
using namespace std;

// Function declaration (prototype)
int square(int num);

int main() {
    int number = 5;
    cout << "The square of " << number << " is " << square(number) << endl;
    return 0;
}

// Function definition
int square(int num) {
    return num * num;
}
```

Explanation:

The function square is declared before its use in main().

Its definition later provides the actual logic.

This separation allows the compiler to understand the function's interface and makes your code modular.

2.3.2 Benefits of Using Functions

Functions offer many advantages:

Reusability: Write the logic once and call it whenever needed.

Modularity: Divide large programs into smaller, manageable parts.

Maintainability: Changes to a function's logic need to be made only in one place.

Testing: Functions can be individually tested for correctness.

2.3.3 Scope and Lifetime of Variables

Variables declared within a function are local to that function. This concept, known as **scope**, helps prevent unintended side effects. Global variables exist outside of functions but should be used sparingly to maintain code clarity.

2.4 Integrating Control Structures and Functions

The true power of C++ emerges when you combine these constructs. A well-designed program might use loops to gather user input, conditionals to decide what to do with that input, and functions to process it. This modular approach not only makes your code more readable but also significantly simplifies debugging and future enhancements.

In summary, this section has provided you with the theoretical framework necessary to use control structures and functions effectively in your C++ programs. With these concepts firmly in hand, you are now ready to set up your development environment and start writing code.

3: Tools and Setup

Before you can put theory into practice, it is vital to configure your development environment properly. In this section, we'll cover the tools, platforms, and step-by-step instructions necessary to get you up and running with C++ programming.

3.1 Choosing the Right Development Environment

For beginners, selecting an Integrated Development Environment (IDE) or a robust text editor is key to a smooth learning experience. Popular options include:

Visual Studio Code (VS Code):

A lightweight, cross-platform editor with a rich ecosystem of extensions for C++.

Code::Blocks:
A free and open-source IDE specifically tailored for C++ development.

CLion:
A professional-grade IDE from JetBrains that offers advanced code analysis and refactoring tools (requires a license for full features).

Visual Studio (Windows):

A comprehensive IDE with a powerful debugger and integrated tools for C++.

Tip: For a beginner-friendly setup, VS Code or Code::Blocks is highly recommended due to their simplicity and extensive community support.

3.2 Installing a Compiler

C++ is a compiled language, so you will need a compiler. Here's how to install one on various operating systems:

Windows: Installing MinGW (GCC)

Download and Install:

Visit MinGW-w64 and follow the installation instructions.

Configure Environment Variables:

Add the MinGW bin directory to your PATH. For example, open Command Prompt and run:

shell

set PATH=%PATH%;C:\MinGW\bin

Verify Installation:

Type:

shell

g++ --version

to ensure GCC is installed.

macOS: Installing Xcode Command Line Tools

Open Terminal:

Launch Terminal from Applications > Utilities.

Install Tools:

Run:

shell

xcode-select --install

Verify Installation:

Confirm by typing:

shell

gcc --version

Linux: Installing GCC

For Debian/Ubuntu systems, run:

shell

sudo apt update

sudo apt install build-essential

3.3 Configuring Your IDE

After installing your compiler, configure your chosen IDE:

Project Organization:

Create a directory structure to organize your projects. For example:

css

CppProjects/

├── TemperatureConverter/

| ├── main.cpp

| ├── converter.h

| └── converter.cpp

Editor Preferences:

Set up code formatting rules (indentation, font size, themes) to make reading and writing code easier.

Version Control:

Install Git and set up a repository (e.g., on GitHub) to track changes and collaborate if desired.

3.4 Verifying Your Environment

To verify your setup, create a simple "Hello, World!" program (if you haven't already) and compile it. For example:

```cpp
#include <iostream>
using namespace std;

int main() {
    cout << "Hello, World!" << endl;
    return 0;
}
```

Compile and run the program. If you see the expected output, your environment is properly configured and you're ready to move on to more complex projects.

4: Hands-on Examples & Projects

Now that you've established a solid foundation of theory and set up your development environment, it's time to roll up your sleeves and put these concepts into practice. In this section, we'll guide you through several practical examples. We begin with a detailed walkthrough of the Temperature Converter project—a real-world application that utilizes conditionals, loops, and functions.

4.1 Project Overview: Temperature Converter

The Temperature Converter is a console-based application that converts temperatures between Celsius and Fahrenheit. This project will help you understand:

Using Conditionals: To determine which conversion to apply.

Using Loops: To allow the user to perform multiple conversions until they choose to exit.

Creating and Using Functions: To encapsulate the conversion logic and keep your code modular.

4.2 Setting Up the Project Files

Organize your project into three main files:

main.cpp: Contains the main() function and handles user interaction.

converter.h: Contains function declarations for temperature conversion.

converter.cpp: Contains function definitions.

4.2.1 File: converter.h

```cpp
cpp
// converter.h: Contains function declarations for
temperature conversion

#ifndef CONVERTER_H
#define CONVERTER_H

// Converts Celsius to Fahrenheit
double celsiusToFahrenheit(double celsius);

// Converts Fahrenheit to Celsius
double fahrenheitToCelsius(double fahrenheit);

#endif // CONVERTER_H
```

4.2.2 File: converter.cpp

```cpp
cpp
// converter.cpp: Contains function definitions for
temperature conversion
#include "converter.h"
```

```cpp
// Convert Celsius to Fahrenheit using the formula: F = (C
* 9/5) + 32
double celsiusToFahrenheit(double celsius) {
    return (celsius * 9.0 / 5.0) + 32;
}

// Convert Fahrenheit to Celsius using the formula: C = (F
- 32) * 5/9
double fahrenheitToCelsius(double fahrenheit) {
    return (fahrenheit - 32) * 5.0 / 9.0;
}
```

4.2.3 File: main.cpp

```cpp
cpp
// main.cpp: Main program for the Temperature Converter
#include <iostream>
#include "converter.h"

using namespace std;

int main() {
    char choice;

    double temperature, convertedTemp;
    do {
        // Display the menu
        cout << "Temperature Converter" << endl;
        cout << "---------------------" << endl;
        cout << "Choose an option:" << endl;
        cout << "1. Convert Celsius to Fahrenheit" << endl;
        cout << "2. Convert Fahrenheit to Celsius" << endl;
        cout << "Q. Quit" << endl;
        cout << "Enter your choice: ";
        cin >> choice;
```

```cpp
    // Process the user's choice using conditionals
    if (choice == '1') (
        cout << "Enter temperature in Celsius: ";
        cin >> temperature;
        convertedTemp = celsiusToFahrenheit(temperature);
        cout << temperature << "°C is " << convertedTemp <<
"°F" << endl;
    ) else if (choice == '2') (
        cout << "Enter temperature in Fahrenheit: ";
        cin >> temperature;
        convertedTemp = fahrenheitToCelsius(temperature);
        cout << temperature << "°F is " << convertedTemp <<
"°C" << endl;
    ) else if (choice == 'Q' || choice == 'q') (
        cout << "Exiting the converter. Goodbye!" << endl;
    ) else (
        cout << "Invalid option. Please try again." << endl;
    )
    cout << endl; // Blank line for readability
    ) while (choice != 'Q' && choice != 'q');

    return 0;
)
```

4.3 Compiling and Running the Project

To compile the project from the command line, navigate to the project directory and run:

shell

```
g++ -o TemperatureConverter main.cpp converter.cpp
```

Then, run the executable:

shell

```
./TemperatureConverter
```

Test the application by selecting various options and inputting different temperature values. The program should correctly convert and display the results, looping until you choose to quit.

4.4 Enhancing the Temperature Converter

Now that you have a basic converter working, consider these enhancements:

Input Validation:

Validate that the user's temperature input is numeric and within a reasonable range.

Additional Conversion Options:

Expand the menu to include Kelvin or Rankine conversions.

Improved User Interface:

Add clearer prompts or even graphical elements if you move to a GUI framework later.

4.5 Exploring Loop Variants and Conditionals

Experiment by replacing the do-while loop with a while loop. For example:

```cpp
// Alternative main loop using while
#include <iostream>
#include "converter.h"

using namespace std;

int main() {
    char choice = ' ';
```

```
while (choice != 'Q' && choice != 'q') (
    cout << "Temperature Converter" << endl;
    // (Menu and processing as before)
    // ...
)
return 0;
)
```

This exercise will help you understand the nuances between loop types and their appropriate use cases.

4.6 Best Practices in Coding Projects

Comment Liberally:

Ensure every function, loop, and conditional is well-commented.

Modularize Code:

As shown, separate conversion logic into its own module.

Consistent Formatting:

Use a consistent coding style to improve readability and maintenance.

Before-and-After Example:

Before:
A single monolithic file mixing user interaction and conversion logic.

After:

The modular structure with main.cpp, converter.h, and converter.cpp separating concerns.

Throughout this section, we have walked through the entire process of developing a complete application using control structures and functions. This Temperature Converter project not only demonstrates your grasp of theory but also shows how to apply these concepts to solve practical problems.

5: Advanced Techniques & Optimization

As you grow more comfortable with control structures and functions, it's time to explore advanced techniques and optimization strategies that can further enhance your code's performance and maintainability.

5.1 Advanced Conditional Structures

5.1.1 Ternary Operators

For simple conditional assignments, the ternary operator offers a concise syntax:

```cpp
int maxVal = (a > b) ? a : b;
```

This single line replaces a multi-line if-else structure when the logic is simple.

5.1.2 Nested and Compound Conditionals

While nesting conditionals can sometimes reduce readability, there are scenarios where compound conditionals (using logical operators such as && and ||) are more efficient.

5.2 Loop Optimization Strategies

5.2.1 Loop Unrolling

In performance-critical applications, manually unrolling loops can reduce the overhead of loop control. However, use this sparingly, as modern compilers often perform unrolling automatically.

5.2.2 Efficient Iteration

When iterating over containers (e.g., vectors or arrays), consider using iterators or range-based for loops for improved clarity and performance:

```cpp
#include <vector>
#include <iostream>
```

```
using namespace std;

int main() {
    vector<int> numbers = {1, 2, 3, 4, 5};
    for (const auto &num : numbers) {
        cout << num << " ";
    }
    cout << endl;
    return 0;
}
```

5.3 Function Optimization Techniques

5.3.1 Inlining Functions

For small, frequently called functions, you can suggest to the compiler to inline them:

cpp

```
inline double add(double a, double b) {
    return a + b;
}
```

Inlining can eliminate the overhead of a function call, although the compiler makes the final decision.

5.3.2 Recursion vs. Iteration

Understand when to use recursion and when an iterative approach is more efficient. In many cases, loops are preferable due to lower overhead.

5.4 Memory and Resource Management

Even though our projects are simple, learning best practices in memory management early on is beneficial:

Pass by Reference:

Avoid unnecessary ing by passing large objects by reference.

Const Correctness:

Use the const keyword where appropriate to prevent unintended modifications.

5.5 Best Practices for Future Code Maintenance

Modular Code Design:

Continue to break your code into small, testable functions.

Documentation:
Maintain thorough documentation and comments to help future you (or other developers) understand your code quickly.

Use Profiling Tools:

Tools like gprof or Valgrind can help you identify performance bottlenecks.

By integrating these advanced techniques into your workflow, you can write code that is not only correct but also optimized for performance and scalability.

6: Troubleshooting and Problem-Solving

Every programmer faces challenges. This section provides strategies and tips to troubleshoot common issues when working with control structures and functions.

6.1 Common Pitfalls

6.1.1 Syntax Errors

Often, missing semicolons or mismatched braces cause compilation errors. Always carefully read compiler error messages—they usually indicate exactly where the problem is.

6.1.2 Logical Errors

Even if your code compiles, logical errors (such as incorrect loop conditions or faulty conditional logic) can lead to unexpected results. Use print statements or a debugger to track variable values.

6.1.3 Function Mismatch Errors

Ensure that your function declarations in header files match their definitions exactly in terms of return type and parameters.

Before-and-After Example:

Before: A header file declaring a function with an int parameter but the definition uses a double parameter.

After: Correctly matching both declaration and definition.

6.2 Debugging Techniques

6.2.1 Print Debugging

Insert cout statements to print variable values at key points in your code. This is a simple yet effective debugging strategy.

6.2.2 Using a Debugger

Tools such as GDB allow you to set breakpoints, step through your code, and inspect variables. For example, compile with debugging symbols:

shell

g++ -g -o TemperatureConverter main.cpp converter.cpp

gdb TemperatureConverter

6.2.3 Verbose Compilation

Compile your code with the -Wall flag to enable all warnings, helping you catch potential issues early.

6.3 Handling User Input Errors

Validate user input to avoid crashes or logic errors:

Check that numeric inputs are valid.

Use conditionals to handle unexpected input gracefully.

6.4 Developing a Systematic Problem-Solving Mindset

Isolate the Issue:

Comment out or simplify sections of your code to pinpoint the source of an error.

Search for Solutions:

Use online communities like Stack Overflow when stuck.

Document Your Fixes:

Keep a log of common errors and how you resolved them for future reference.

By following these troubleshooting strategies, you'll be better equipped to handle the inevitable challenges that come with programming.

7: Conclusion & Next Steps

Congratulations on completing this in-depth chapter on control structures and functions! You've learned how to guide the flow of your C++ programs using conditionals and loops, and how to break your code into manageable, reusable functions. The Temperature Converter project has given you practical experience in applying these concepts to create a real-world application.

7.1 Recap of Key Points

Control Structures:

You now understand how to use if-else statements, switch cases, and various loops (for, while, do-while) to control program execution.

Functions:
You learned the importance of modularizing code through functions, how to declare and define them, and how they promote code reusability and clarity.

Project Application:

The Temperature Converter project served as a practical example that integrated all these concepts into one cohesive program.

7.2 Reflecting on Your Learning

As you reflect on what you have learned in this chapter, consider how the principles of control flow and modular design apply to all areas of programming. Whether you are processing user input, handling data structures, or building complex systems, the techniques covered here are universally applicable.

7.3 Next Steps in Your C++ Journey

Now that you have a solid foundation:

Practice:
Continue to build small projects that incorporate conditionals, loops, and functions. Experiment with modifying the Temperature Converter or create your own application.

Deepen Your Knowledge:

Explore advanced topics such as recursion, function overloading, lambda expressions, and more sophisticated control flow constructs.

Engage with the Community:

Join forums, contribute to open-source projects, and participate in coding meetups to exchange ideas and learn from others.

7.4 Additional Resources

For further learning, consider these resources:

Books:

"C++ Primer" by Stanley B. Lippman, Josée Lajoie, and Barbara E. Moo

"Effective C++" by Scott Meyers

Websites:

cppreference.com for detailed documentation

LearnCPP.com for tutorials and exercises

Online Courses:

Look for interactive courses that provide hands-on challenges and real-world projects.

7.5 Final Words of Encouragement

Remember, every great programmer started exactly where you are now. The concepts you've mastered in this chapter are the stepping stones to writing efficient, scalable, and maintainable software. As you continue to experiment, build projects, and refine your skills, you'll find that the once-challenging world of programming gradually becomes second nature.

Embrace each challenge as an opportunity to learn and grow. With persistence, curiosity, and a commitment to continuous improvement, you'll unlock the full potential of C++ and transform your ideas into powerful applications.

CHAPTER 5: ARRAYS, STRINGS, AND COLLECTIONS

1 Introduction

Welcome to Chapter 5! In this chapter, we dive into one of the most essential aspects of programming: managing collections of data. Whether you are storing a series of temperatures, names, or any other kind of data, arrays, strings, and collections are at the heart of it all. You will learn how to work with arrays and vectors, manipulate strings, and apply these concepts to build a practical, real-world project—the Contact List Manager.

Why Arrays, Strings, and Collections Matter

In nearly every programming task, data storage and manipulation are critical. Arrays provide the simplest way to store a sequence of elements in contiguous memory, while vectors (the dynamic array in C++) offer flexibility when the number of elements isn't known in advance. Strings—collections of characters—are used to store textual data, and understanding how to work with them is key to almost every application you will ever develop.

Imagine you are creating an application to manage your contacts. You need to store names, phone numbers, and email addresses in a way that allows for quick access, easy updating, and efficient searching. By mastering arrays, vectors, and strings, you lay the groundwork for building applications that can manage large amounts of data with ease and speed.

Key Concepts and Terminology

Throughout this chapter, you will become familiar with several important concepts:

Arrays: Fixed-size, contiguous blocks of memory for storing elements of the same data type.

Vectors: Dynamic arrays provided by the C++ Standard Template Library (STL) that can change size during runtime.

Strings: Sequences of characters that represent textual data.

Collections: A general term for data structures that hold groups of elements (including arrays, vectors, lists, etc.).

Basic String Manipulation: Operations such as concatenation, comparison, and substring extraction.

Setting the Tone

Our goal in this chapter is to build your confidence in working with collections of data. We will start by exploring the theory behind arrays, vectors, and strings, using real-world analogies to make abstract ideas tangible. Then, we will move into hands-on examples, where you'll see clean, well-documented code that demonstrates how to manipulate these data structures. Finally, you will apply everything you've learned in a hands-on project—a Contact List Manager—that simulates a real-world application.

By the end of this chapter, you will have a deep understanding of how to use arrays, strings, and collections effectively. You'll be well-prepared to build applications that require robust data management and manipulation. Let's begin our journey into the world of arrays, strings, and collections!

2. Core Concepts and Theory

In this section, we will explore the theoretical underpinnings of arrays, strings, and collections in C++. Understanding these core concepts will help you appreciate their strengths and limitations, and it will form the basis for writing efficient, maintainable code.

2.1 Working with Arrays

2.1.1 Definition and Characteristics

An array is a collection of elements of the same type stored in contiguous memory. Because arrays have a fixed size determined at compile time, they offer fast access (via indices) but lack flexibility when it comes to resizing.

Key Characteristics:

Fixed Size: The size of an array must be known at compile time.

Contiguous Memory: Arrays allocate a continuous block of memory, making element access very efficient.

Indexing: Elements are accessed via zero-based indices.

Example:

```cpp
#include <iostream>
using namespace std;

int main() {
    int numbers[5] = {10, 20, 30, 40, 50};
    cout << "The third element is: " << numbers[2] << endl; // Outputs 30
    return 0;
}
```

2.1.2 Advantages and Limitations

Advantages:

Fast element access using indices.

Low memory overhead due to contiguous storage.

Limitations:

Fixed size; resizing requires creating a new array.

Lack of built-in methods for common operations (e.g., insertion, deletion).

2.2 Vectors: Dynamic Arrays

2.2.1 Introduction to Vectors

Vectors are part of the C++ STL and provide a dynamic array that can resize automatically. They combine the speed of arrays with the flexibility of dynamic memory allocation.

Example:

```cpp
cpp
#include <iostream>
#include <vector>
using namespace std;

int main() {
    vector<int> numbers = (10, 20, 30, 40, 50);
    numbers.push_back(60); // Adds 60 to the end of the vector
    cout << "Vector size: " << numbers.size() << endl;
    cout << "Last element: " << numbers(numbers.size()-1) << endl;
    return 0;
}
```

2.2.2 Advantages of Vectors

Dynamic Resizing: Automatically adjusts size as elements are added or removed.

Rich Library Support: Comes with a variety of methods (e.g., push_back, pop_back, insert, erase).

Ease of Use: Provides bounds checking (with methods like at()) and iterators for traversal.

2.3 Basic String Manipulation

2.3.1 Working with Strings in C++

C++ provides a powerful string class (std::string) that makes working with text easy and intuitive. Unlike C-style strings (character arrays), std::string objects are dynamic and come with a plethora of built-in methods.

Example:

```cpp
#include <iostream>
#include <string>
using namespace std;

int main() {
    string greeting = "Hello, World!";
    cout << greeting << endl;
    cout << "The length of the greeting is: " << greeting.length() << endl;
    return 0;
}
```

2.3.2 Common String Operations

Concatenation: Joining two or more strings.

```cpp
string firstName = "John";
string lastName = "Doe";
string fullName = firstName + " " + lastName;
```

Substring Extraction: Extracting a portion of a string.

```cpp
string sub = fullName.substr(0, 4); // "John"
```

Searching: Finding the position of a substring.

```cpp
size_t pos = fullName.find("Doe");
if (pos != string::npos) {
    cout << "Found at position: " << pos << endl;
```

)

2.4 Collections in C++ Beyond Arrays and Vectors

While arrays and vectors are among the most common collections, the STL provides many other containers, such as lists, sets, and maps. In this chapter, however, we focus on arrays, vectors, and strings, as they form the core building blocks for many applications.

2.5 Real-World Analogies

Imagine a library:

Arrays: A fixed shelf with a set number of books.

Vectors: A flexible bookshelf that can expand as new books are added.

Strings: The titles of books, which can be manipulated, combined, or searched for specific words.

These analogies help illustrate the concepts behind these data structures and emphasize their roles in storing and managing data.

3. Tools and Setup

Before we get into coding, let's set up the tools and environment you'll need to work comfortably with arrays, strings, and collections in C++. This section covers the selection of an IDE, installing the compiler, and configuring your project workspace.

3.1 Choosing an IDE or Text Editor

For beginners and hobbyists, a friendly and robust development environment is key. Here are some popular options:

Visual Studio Code (VS Code):

A lightweight editor with extensive extensions for C++ (e.g., the C/C++ extension by Microsoft).

Code::Blocks:
An open-source, beginner-friendly IDE that supports C++ out of the box.

CLion:
A professional-grade IDE from JetBrains offering advanced features like code analysis and refactoring (note that it requires a license).

Visual Studio (Windows):

A comprehensive IDE that includes powerful debugging and project management tools.

Tip: If you're just starting, VS Code or Code::Blocks are excellent choices due to their simplicity and strong community support.

3.2 Installing a Compiler

C++ is a compiled language, so you'll need a C++ compiler. The most common compiler is GCC (GNU Compiler Collection), but alternatives such as Clang or Microsoft's MSVC are also available.

For Windows: Installing MinGW (GCC)

Download MinGW-w64:

Visit the MinGW-w64 website and download the installer.

Install:
Follow the on-screen instructions to install the compiler.

Configure PATH:

Add the path to the MinGW bin directory (e.g., C:\MinGW\bin) to your system's PATH variable.

Verify Installation:

Open Command Prompt and run:

shell

g++ —version

For macOS: Installing Xcode Command Line Tools

Open Terminal:

Navigate to Applications > Utilities > Terminal.

Install Tools:

Run:

shell

xcode-select --install

Verify Installation:

Run:

shell

gcc --version

For Linux: Installing GCC

On Ubuntu or Debian-based systems:

shell

sudo apt update

sudo apt install build-essential

3.3 Configuring Your Project Workspace

Organize your projects in a clear directory structure. For example, for our upcoming Contact List Manager project, you might set up your workspace as follows:

css

CppProjects/

└── **ContactListManager/**

├── **main.cpp**

├── **contact.h**

├── **contact.cpp**

└── **utils.h**

└── **utils.cpp**

3.4 Setting Up Version Control

Using Git for version control is highly recommended:

Install Git:

Download and install Git from git-scm.com.

Create a Repository:

Initialize a repository in your project folder:

shell

git init

Commit Your Code:

Regular commits help track changes and revert to previous states if needed.

3.5 Verifying Your Environment

Before moving on to the hands-on examples, verify that your environment is set up correctly by compiling a simple "Hello, World!" program:

```cpp
#include <iostream>
using namespace std;

int main() (
    cout << "Hello, World!" << endl;
    return 0;
)
```

Compile and run this program to ensure that your IDE, compiler, and Git are functioning as expected.

4. Hands-on Examples & Projects

In this section, we will put theory into practice by building several practical examples that demonstrate how to work with arrays, strings, and collections. The centerpiece of this section is our hands-on project: the Contact List Manager. This project will bring together everything you've learned so far.

4.1 Project Overview: Contact List Manager

The Contact List Manager is a console-based application that allows users to manage a list of contacts. Each contact consists of a name, phone number, and email address. You will use:

Arrays/Vectors: To store and manage the list of contacts.

Strings: To manipulate contact information.

Basic Input/Output: To interact with the user.

Functions: To modularize your code.

4.2 Setting Up the Project Files

For our Contact List Manager, we will create three main files:

main.cpp: Contains the main function and the user interface logic.

contact.h: Declares the Contact structure and function prototypes for contact management.

contact.cpp: Defines the functions for adding, displaying, editing, and deleting contacts.

4.2.1 File: contact.h

```cpp
// contact.h: Contains the definition of the Contact
structure and function declarations

#ifndef CONTACT_H
#define CONTACT_H
```

```cpp
#include <string>
#include <vector>

// Define a Contact structure to hold individual contact
information
struct Contact {
    std::string name;
    std::string phone;
    std::string email;
};

// Function prototypes for contact management
void addContact(std::vector<Contact>& contacts);
void displayContacts(const std::vector<Contact>& contacts);
void editContact(std::vector<Contact>& contacts);
void deleteContact(std::vector<Contact>& contacts);

#endif // CONTACT_H
```

4.2.2 File: contact.cpp

cpp

```cpp
// contact.cpp: Implements functions for managing contacts
#include "contact.h"
#include <iostream>

using namespace std;

// Function to add a new contact
void addContact(vector<Contact>& contacts) {
    Contact newContact;
    cout << "Enter name: ";
    cin.ignore();  // Clear the input buffer
    getline(cin, newContact.name);
```

```cpp
    cout << "Enter phone number: ";
    getline(cin, newContact.phone);
    cout << "Enter email: ";
    getline(cin, newContact.email);
    contacts.push_back(newContact);
    cout << "Contact added successfully." << endl;
}
```

// Function to display all contacts

```cpp
void displayContacts(const vector<Contact>& contacts) {
    if (contacts.empty()) {
        cout << "No contacts to display." << endl;
        return;
    }
    cout << "\nContact List:" << endl;
    for (size_t i = 0; i < contacts.size(); i++) {
        cout << "Contact " << i + 1 << ":" << endl;
        cout << " Name: " << contacts(i).name << endl;
        cout << " Phone: " << contacts(i).phone << endl;
        cout << " Email: " << contacts(i).email << endl;
        cout << "-----------------------------" << endl;
    }
}
```

// **Function to edit an existing contact**

```cpp
void editContact(vector<Contact>& contacts) {
    if (contacts.empty()) {
        cout << "No contacts available to edit." << endl;
        return;
    }
    size_t index;
    cout << "Enter the contact number to edit: ";
    cin >> index;
```

```cpp
    if (index < 1 || index > contacts.size()) {
        cout << "Invalid contact number." << endl;
        return;
    }
    cin.ignore();
    cout << "Editing contact " << index << ":" << endl;
    cout << "Enter new name (or press enter to keep current):
";
    string input;
    getline(cin, input);
    if (!input.empty())
        contacts(index - 1).name = input;
    cout << "Enter new phone (or press enter to keep current):
";
    getline(cin, input);
    if (!input.empty())
        contacts(index - 1).phone = input;
    cout << "Enter new email (or press enter to keep current):
";
    getline(cin, input);
    if (!input.empty())
        contacts(index - 1).email = input;
    cout << "Contact updated successfully." << endl;
}


// Function to delete a contact
void deleteContact(vector<Contact>& contacts) {
    if (contacts.empty()) {
        cout << "No contacts available to delete." << endl;
        return;
    }
    size_t index;
    cout << "Enter the contact number to delete: ";
```

```cpp
        cin >> index;
        if (index < 1 || index > contacts.size()) {
            cout << "Invalid contact number." << endl;
            return;
        }
        contacts.erase(contacts.begin() + index - 1);
        cout << "Contact deleted successfully." << endl;
}
```

4.2.3 File: main.cpp

```cpp
cpp
// main.cpp: Main program for the Contact List Manager
#include <iostream>
#include <vector>
#include "contact.h"


using namespace std;


int main() {
    vector<Contact> contacts;
    char choice;
    do {
        cout << "\nContact List Manager" << endl;
        cout << "---------------------" << endl;
        cout << "1. Add Contact" << endl;
        cout << "2. Display Contacts" << endl;
        cout << "3. Edit Contact" << endl;
        cout << "4. Delete Contact" << endl;
        cout << "Q. Quit" << endl;
        cout << "Enter your choice: ";
        cin >> choice;
```

```
switch (choice) (
    case '1':
       addContact(contacts);
       break;
    case '2':
       displayContacts(contacts);
       break;
    case '3':
       editContact(contacts);
       break;
    case '4':
       deleteContact(contacts);
       break;
    case 'Q':
    case 'q':
       cout << "Exiting Contact List Manager. Goodbye!"
<< endl;
       break;
    default:
       cout << "Invalid option. Please try again." <<
endl;
    )
  ) while (choice != 'Q' && choice != 'q');

    return 0;
)
```

4.3 Compiling and Running the Contact List Manager

Compilation:
Open your terminal in the project directory and compile the project:

shell

```
g++ -o ContactListManager main.cpp contact.cpp
```

Execution:
Run the executable:

```
shell
```

```
./ContactListManager
```

Testing:
Test each functionality—adding, displaying, editing, and deleting contacts. Verify that changes persist correctly during the session.

4.4 Enhancing the Project

Once you have the basic functionality working, consider enhancing the Contact List Manager:

Input Validation:

Ensure that fields such as phone number and email are validated.

Persistent Storage:

Extend the project to read from and write to a file so contacts are saved between sessions.

User Interface Improvements:

Add clearer prompts and error messages, or even migrate to a graphical user interface (GUI) using libraries like Qt.

4.5 Additional Practical Examples

To further reinforce your understanding of arrays, strings, and collections, try these additional exercises:

Sorting Contacts:

Implement a function to sort contacts alphabetically by name.

Searching Contacts:

Add functionality to search for a contact by name or phone number.

Batch Updates:

Use loops to allow the user to perform operations on multiple contacts at once.

By completing these hands-on projects, you'll gain practical experience with data collections and understand how to structure your code in a modular, maintainable way.

5. Advanced Techniques & Optimization

As you become more comfortable with the basics, it's time to explore advanced techniques and optimization strategies for working with arrays, strings, and collections. This section will cover best practices, performance optimization tips, and advanced code strategies that can help you write more efficient and scalable applications.

5.1 Advanced Array and Vector Operations

5.1.1 Iterators and Range-Based Loops

Learn how to traverse vectors using iterators or range-based for loops:

```cpp
#include <iostream>
#include <vector>
using namespace std;

int main() {
    vector<int> numbers = {1, 2, 3, 4, 5};
    for (const auto &num : numbers) {
        cout << num << " ";
    }
    cout << endl;
```

```
    return 0;
)
```

Range-based loops improve code clarity and reduce errors associated with index management.

5.1.2 Memory Optimization

For large collections, minimize unnecessary ing:

Pass vectors by reference.

Use move semantics (e.g., std::move) when appropriate.

5.2 Advanced String Manipulation

5.2.1 Regular Expressions

C++ supports regular expressions via <regex>, which can simplify complex string parsing tasks.

```cpp
cpp
#include <iostream>
#include <regex>
#include <string>
using namespace std;

int main() (
    string email = "example@example.com";
    regex emailPattern(R"((\w+)(\.\w+)*@(\w+)(\.\w+)+)");
    if (regex_match(email, emailPattern))
        cout << "Valid email address." << endl;
    else
        cout << "Invalid email address." << endl;
    return 0;
)
```

5.2.2 String Streams

Use string streams for converting between strings and other data types:

```cpp
#include <iostream>
#include <sstream>
#include <string>
using namespace std;

int main() {
    int number = 42;
    ostringstream oss;
    oss << "The answer is " << number;
    string result = oss.str();
    cout << result << endl;
    return 0;
}
```

5.3 Optimization Techniques for Collections

5.3.1 Algorithm Optimization

Leverage STL algorithms (e.g., std::sort, std::find) to perform operations on collections efficiently:

```cpp
#include <iostream>
#include <vector>
#include <algorithm>
using namespace std;

int main() {
    vector<int> numbers = (5, 3, 8, 1, 2);
    sort(numbers.begin(), numbers.end());
```

```
for (const auto &num : numbers)
    cout << num << " ";
cout << endl;
return 0;
)
```

5.3.2 Avoiding Unnecessary Overhead

Optimize by:

Minimizing copies through references.

Using reserve() for vectors when the number of elements is known in advance.

5.4 Best Practices for Advanced Code

Modularization:
Continue to separate code into functions and modules.

Code Readability:

Follow consistent naming conventions and add thorough documentation.

Profiling:
Use profiling tools like gprof or Valgrind to identify bottlenecks.

By applying these advanced techniques, you ensure that your applications not only function correctly but also perform efficiently and scale well as they grow.

6. Troubleshooting and Problem-Solving

Even the best-written code may encounter issues. In this section, we address common pitfalls, provide troubleshooting strategies, and offer guidance on debugging complex problems in array and string manipulation.

6.1 Common Challenges

6.1.1 Out-of-Bounds Errors

When working with arrays or vectors, attempting to access an element outside the valid range is a frequent error. Always validate indices:

cpp

```
if (index >= 0 && index < numbers.size()) (
    // safe to access numbers(index)
)
```

6.1.2 Memory Leaks

Although vectors manage memory automatically, improper use of dynamic memory (if using raw arrays) can cause leaks. Prefer STL containers over raw pointers whenever possible.

6.2 Debugging Techniques

6.2.1 Compiler Warnings

Compile with the -Wall flag to enable warnings. They often hint at potential issues:

shell

```
g++ -Wall -o ContactListManager main.cpp contact.cpp
```

6.2.2 Using a Debugger

Tools like GDB help step through code:

shell

```
g++ -g -o ContactListManager main.cpp contact.cpp
gdb ContactListManager
```

Set breakpoints and inspect variable states to pinpoint errors.

6.3 Troubleshooting Input and Parsing Issues

If your string manipulations or user input functions aren't working as expected:

Check for buffer issues (use cin.ignore() when necessary).

Validate input using conditionals before processing.

6.4 Documenting and Learning from Errors

Maintain a log of common issues and their fixes. This practice not only speeds up future troubleshooting but also deepens your understanding of the language.

7. Conclusion & Next Steps

Congratulations! In this chapter, you have delved into the world of arrays, strings, and collections—key components of C++ programming. You learned about the fundamentals of fixed arrays and dynamic vectors, mastered basic string manipulation techniques, and applied your knowledge by building a practical Contact List Manager.

7.1 Recap of Key Points

Arrays:
Understand fixed-size data storage with fast access, along with its limitations.

Vectors:
Gain flexibility with dynamic arrays that adjust their size automatically.

Strings:
Manipulate text effortlessly using the powerful std::string class and its rich set of functions.

Project Application:

The Contact List Manager project showcased how to integrate arrays, strings, and vectors into a real-world application with user-friendly functionality.

7.2 Reflecting on Your Learning

Consider how the techniques learned in this chapter apply to broader programming challenges. Whether managing user data, processing large datasets, or developing dynamic applications, arrays, vectors, and strings form the backbone of efficient data management. The modular approach you practiced—separating logic into functions and organizing data into collections—will serve you well as you move on to more advanced topics.

7.3 Next Steps in Your C++ Journey

Practice Regularly:

Continue to build projects that involve data collection and manipulation. Experiment with different STL containers to broaden your understanding.

Deepen Your Knowledge:

Explore more advanced topics such as multi-dimensional arrays, string streams, and further STL collections like maps and sets.

Engage with the Community:

Participate in coding forums, contribute to open-source projects, and collaborate with peers to learn new techniques and best practices.

7.4 Additional Resources

For further learning, consider these resources:

Books:

"C++ Primer" by Stanley B. Lippman, Josée Lajoie, and Barbara E. Moo

"Effective STL" by Scott Meyers

Websites:

cppreference.com for in-depth documentation

LearnCPP.com for tutorials and exercises

Online Courses:

Look for interactive courses and challenges that reinforce practical skills.

7.5 Final Words of Encouragement

Mastering arrays, strings, and collections is a milestone in your C++ journey. Every program you write that processes data—no matter how small—relies on these fundamental techniques. As you continue to build and refine your projects, remember that each bug you fix and each optimization you implement makes you a better programmer. Stay curious, keep experimenting, and always strive to write clean, efficient, and maintainable code.

CHAPTER 6: POINTERS AND MEMORY MANAGEMENT

1. Introduction

In any programming language that gives you low-level control over memory, pointers are both a powerful tool and a source of many common pitfalls. In C++, understanding pointers and memory management is essential if you want to write efficient, high-performance software. In this chapter, we will explore the fundamentals of pointers and references, delve into the nuances of dynamic memory allocation using the new and delete operators, and build a project—a Memory Puzzle Game—that brings these concepts to life in a fun and practical way.

Why Pointers and Memory Management Matter

At the heart of C++ lies its ability to give you direct control over memory. Unlike many higher-level languages, C++ lets you manipulate memory directly, which can lead to extremely efficient programs if done correctly. Pointers are variables that store memory addresses, and by mastering them, you unlock the ability to:

Manage dynamic data structures such as linked lists, trees, and graphs.

Optimize performance-critical applications by controlling exactly how and when memory is allocated and deallocated.

Interface with hardware and system resources where direct memory access is crucial.

However, with great power comes great responsibility. Improper use of pointers can result in issues like memory leaks, dangling pointers, and segmentation faults—common sources of bugs in C++ programs. This chapter aims to demystify pointers and memory management, providing you with the knowledge and tools to use them safely and effectively.

Key Concepts and Terminology

Before we dive deeper, let's clarify some key terms:

Pointer: A variable that holds the memory address of another variable.

Reference: An alias for another variable, introduced to simplify pointer usage in many cases.

Dynamic Memory Allocation: The process of allocating memory at runtime using new and deallocating it using delete.

Dangling Pointer: A pointer that references deallocated memory.

Memory Leak: Memory that is allocated but never deallocated, leading to wasted resources.

Setting the Tone

Throughout this chapter, our goal is to strike a balance between theory and practical application. We begin by building a solid theoretical foundation for understanding pointers and dynamic memory. Then, through a series of detailed examples and a comprehensive project—the Memory Puzzle Game—we'll show you how these concepts are applied in real-world scenarios. Our approach is professional yet accessible, ensuring that even if pointers seem daunting at first, you'll soon find them a powerful ally in your programming toolkit.

By the end of this chapter, you will not only understand how pointers work but also how to manage memory dynamically and safely. You'll be well-prepared to tackle more advanced topics in C++ and build robust applications. Let's begin our journey into the intricate world of pointers and memory management!

2. Core Concepts and Theory

This section dives deep into the core concepts of pointers and memory management. We'll cover the fundamentals of pointers and references, explain pointer arithmetic, and discuss the differences between stack and heap memory. We'll then move on to dynamic memory allocation—examining how to allocate and deallocate memory safely using the new and delete operators.

2.1 Understanding Pointers and References

2.1.1 What Are Pointers?

A pointer in C++ is a variable that stores the memory address of another variable. Consider this simple example:

```cpp
#include <iostream>
using namespace std;

int main() (
    int num = 42;      // regular integer variable
    int *ptr = &num;    // pointer variable that stores the
address of num

    cout << "Value of num: " << num << endl;
    cout << "Address of num: " << &num << endl;
    cout << "Value stored in ptr: " << ptr << endl;
    cout << "Value pointed to by ptr: " << *ptr << endl; //
dereferencing
    return 0;
)
```

Explanation:

int *ptr declares a pointer to an integer.

&num retrieves the address of num.

*ptr dereferences the pointer to access the value stored at that address.

2.1.2 Pointer Arithmetic

Pointer arithmetic allows you to navigate through arrays or contiguous memory blocks. For example, if you have an array, a pointer to its first element can be incremented to access subsequent elements:

```cpp
#include <iostream>
using namespace std;

int main() (
    int arr(5) = (10, 20, 30, 40, 50);
    int *p = arr;  // equivalent to int *p = &arr(0);

    for (int i = 0; i < 5; i++) (
        cout << "Element " << i << ": " << *(p + i) << endl;
    )
    return 0;
)
```

Key Points:

Adding an integer to a pointer moves it by that many elements.

This is particularly useful for iterating over arrays.

2.1.3 References as an Alternative

A reference is an alias for another variable. Unlike pointers, references cannot be null and do not support pointer arithmetic. They are typically used to pass variables to functions without ing them.

```cpp
#include <iostream>
using namespace std;

void increment(int &ref) (
    ref++;
)

int main() (
```

```cpp
int num = 10;
increment(num);
cout << "Incremented num: " << num << endl;  // Outputs
11
return 0;
)
```

Advantages of References:

Simplifies syntax: no need for dereferencing.

Ensures that a valid variable is always referenced.

2.2 Memory Management in C++

C++ provides both automatic (stack) and manual (heap) memory management. Understanding the difference is crucial for writing efficient programs.

2.2.1 The Stack vs. the Heap

Stack Memory:

Used for static memory allocation (e.g., local variables). It is managed automatically, with memory being freed when a function exits. Stack memory is fast but limited in size.

Heap Memory:

Used for dynamic memory allocation. Memory is allocated and freed explicitly by the programmer using new and delete. The heap is larger than the stack but slower due to fragmentation and manual management.

2.2.2 Dynamic Memory Allocation: new and delete

Dynamic memory allocation in C++ is performed using the new operator, which allocates memory on the heap, and the delete operator, which frees that memory.

Example:

```cpp
cpp
#include <iostream>
using namespace std;
```

```
int main() {
   int *ptr = new int;    // dynamically allocate an integer
   *ptr = 100;            // assign a value
   cout << "Value: " << *ptr << endl;
   delete ptr;            // free the memory

   // Allocating an array dynamically
   int *arr = new int(5);
   for (int i = 0; i < 5; i++) {
      arr(i) = i * 10;
   }
   for (int i = 0; i < 5; i++) {
      cout << "arr(" << i << "): " << arr(i) << endl;
   }
   delete() arr;          // free the array memory
   return 0;
}
```

Important Points:

Use delete for single elements and delete[] for arrays.

Failing to free allocated memory leads to memory leaks.

Always initialize pointers and set them to nullptr after deletion.

2.3 Pointers, References, and Memory Management Together

Combining these concepts allows you to build dynamic data structures such as linked lists, trees, and graphs. Understanding how pointers interact with memory and how to manage that memory safely is essential for advanced C++ programming.

Real-World Analogy:

Consider dynamic memory as renting an apartment. You use new to rent a space (allocate memory) and delete to vacate it (free memory). If you forget to vacate, you end up paying rent (memory leak) for a space you no longer use.

2.4 Summary of Core Theory

By now, you should have a clear understanding of:

Pointers: Their declaration, dereferencing, and arithmetic.

References: A safer, simpler alternative for passing variables.

Dynamic Memory Allocation: How to allocate and deallocate memory with new and delete.

Stack vs. Heap: The differences between automatic and dynamic memory.

These fundamentals are critical as we move on to hands-on projects that require you to manage memory explicitly.

3. Tools and Setup

To effectively work with pointers and memory management, you need a properly configured development environment and the right tools. In this section, we'll guide you through selecting an IDE, installing a compiler, and configuring debugging tools to help you catch memory-related issues.

3.1 Choosing an IDE or Text Editor

For C++ development, especially when dealing with pointers, a robust IDE can significantly streamline your workflow. Recommended options include:

Visual Studio Code (VS Code):

Lightweight and highly extensible with the C/C++ extension by Microsoft.

Code::Blocks:
An open-source IDE with built-in support for C++ and a user-friendly interface.

CLion:
A professional IDE from JetBrains with advanced debugging and code analysis features.

Visual Studio (Windows):

A comprehensive environment that offers excellent debugging and profiling tools.

Tip: Beginners often find VS Code or Code::Blocks particularly friendly due to their ease of setup and active community support.

3.2 Installing a Compiler

C++ code must be compiled before it can run. The most common compiler is GCC, but you might also choose Clang or MSVC depending on your platform.

For Windows: Installing MinGW (GCC)

Download:
Visit MinGW-w64 and download the installer.

Install:
Follow the installation wizard. Make sure to install the C++ compiler.

Configure PATH:

Add the MinGW bin directory (e.g., C:\MinGW\bin) to your system's PATH variable.

Verify:
Open Command Prompt and run:

shell

g++ --version

For macOS: Installing Xcode Command Line Tools

Open Terminal:

Navigate to Applications > Utilities > Terminal.

Install:
Run:

```shell
xcode-select --install
```
Verify:
Type:

```shell
gcc --version
```

For Linux: Installing GCC

On Ubuntu or Debian-based systems:

```shell
sudo apt update
sudo apt install build-essential
```

3.3 Configuring Debugging and Profiling Tools

Pointers and memory issues can be tricky to debug. Consider these tools:

GDB (GNU Debugger):

Use GDB to set breakpoints, step through your code, and inspect variables.

Valgrind:
An invaluable tool for detecting memory leaks, invalid memory access, and other issues.

IDE Debuggers:

Many IDEs come with integrated debugging tools that visualize memory usage and pointer references.

3.4 Verifying Your Environment

Before diving into more advanced projects, test your setup with a simple program that uses pointers and dynamic memory. For example, compile and run the "Hello, World!" program from earlier. Ensuring that your environment is configured correctly is the first step toward writing robust, memory-safe code.

4. Hands-on Examples & Projects: Memory Puzzle Game

In this section, we will build a project that challenges you to put your pointer and memory management skills to work: the Memory Puzzle Game. This console-based game will require you to manage dynamic memory, use pointers to manipulate game data, and apply careful memory management techniques to avoid leaks and errors.

4.1 Project Overview

The Memory Puzzle Game is a simple game where players must match pairs of hidden items. The game board is stored in dynamic memory, and pointers are used to access and modify the game state. Key features include:

Dynamic allocation of a game board (a 2D array) using new.

Use of pointers to navigate and update the board.

Proper cleanup of memory using delete[].

A game loop that continues until all pairs are found.

4.2 Setting Up Project Files

Organize your project into the following files:

main.cpp: Contains the main function and overall game loop.

game.h: Contains declarations for game functions and data structures.

game.cpp: Implements the game functions, including board initialization, display, input handling, and cleanup.

4.2.1 File: game.h

```cpp
// game.h: Declarations for the Memory Puzzle Game
#ifndef GAME_H
#define GAME_H
```

```cpp
#include <string>

// Function prototypes
char** initializeBoard(int rows, int cols);
void displayBoard(char** board, int rows, int cols);
void playGame(char** board, int rows, int cols);
void cleanupBoard(char** board, int rows);

#endif // GAME_H
```

4.2.2 File: game.cpp

cpp
```cpp
// game.cpp: Implements the Memory Puzzle Game functions
#include "game.h"
#include <iostream>
#include <cstdlib>
#include <ctime>

using namespace std;

// Initialize a dynamic 2D game board with hidden
characters
char** initializeBoard(int rows, int cols) (
    char** board = new char*(rows);
    for (int i = 0; i < rows; i++) (
        board(i) = new char(cols);
    )

    // For simplicity, fill the board with letters (simulate
pairs)
    char letter = 'A';
    for (int i = 0; i < rows; i++) (
        for (int j = 0; j < cols; j += 2) (
```

```cpp
            board(i)(j) = letter;
            board(i)(j + 1) = letter;
            letter++;
            if (letter > 'Z') letter = 'A';
        )
    )
```

// Shuffle the board positions

```cpp
    srand(static_cast<unsigned>(time(0)));
    for (int i = 0; i < rows; i++) (
        for (int j = 0; j < cols; j++) (
            int randRow = rand() % rows;
            int randCol = rand() % cols;
            swap(board(i)(j), board(randRow)(randCol));
        )
    )
    return board;
)
```

// Display the game board (for debugging, show letters; in an actual game, hide unmatched pairs)

```cpp
void displayBoard(char** board, int rows, int cols) (
    for (int i = 0; i < rows; i++) (
        for (int j = 0; j < cols; j++) (
            cout << board(i)(j) << " ";
        )
        cout << endl;
    )
)
```

// Main game loop (simplified for this example)

```cpp
void playGame(char** board, int rows, int cols) (
```

```cpp
    cout << "Welcome to the Memory Puzzle Game!" << endl;
    int moves = 0;
    // In a full game, you would add logic to handle player
input, matching pairs, and hiding/uncovering cells.
    // For brevity, we simply simulate a few moves and then
end the game.
    cout << "Simulating game moves..." << endl;
    moves = 5;
    cout << "Game over! You completed the game in " << moves
<< " moves." << endl;
)
```

// Clean up dynamically allocated memory for the board

```cpp
void cleanupBoard(char** board, int rows) (
    for (int i = 0; i < rows; i++) (
        delete() board(i);
    )
    delete() board;
)
```

4.2.3 File: main.cpp

```cpp
cpp
// main.cpp: Main driver for the Memory Puzzle Game
#include "game.h"
#include <iostream>
using namespace std;

int main() (
    const int rows = 4;
    const int cols = 4;

    // Initialize the game board dynamically
    char** gameBoard = initializeBoard(rows, cols);
```

```
    // Display the board (for demonstration purposes)
    displayBoard(gameBoard, rows, cols);

    // Start the game
    playGame(gameBoard, rows, cols);

    // Clean up allocated memory
    cleanupBoard(gameBoard, rows);

    return 0;
}
```

4.3 Compiling and Running the Project

Compilation:
Open your terminal in the project directory and compile:

shell

g++ -o MemoryPuzzleGame main.cpp game.cpp

Execution:
Run the game:

shell

./MemoryPuzzleGame

Testing:
Verify that the game board displays, that the game simulation runs, and—most importantly—that all dynamically allocated memory is freed when the game ends.

4.4 Expanding the Memory Puzzle Game

Consider enhancements:

User Input:

Allow the user to select board positions to reveal and match pairs.

State Management:

Maintain hidden and revealed states for each cell.

Scorekeeping and Timing:

Track moves and elapsed time.

Graphical Interface:

Integrate with a GUI library (e.g., SFML or Qt) for a more engaging experience.

5. Advanced Techniques & Optimization

Now that you have built a working Memory Puzzle Game and understand the basics of pointers and dynamic memory, we turn our attention to advanced techniques and optimization strategies.

5.1 Advanced Pointer Techniques

5.1.1 Smart Pointers

Modern C++ (C++11 and later) provides smart pointers (e.g., std::unique_ptr, std::shared_ptr) to automatically manage dynamic memory and help prevent leaks.

```cpp
#include <iostream>
#include <memory>
using namespace std;

int main() {
    unique_ptr<int> ptr(new int(42));
    cout << "Value: " << *ptr << endl;
    // No need to call delete; memory is automatically freed when ptr goes out of scope.
    return 0;
}
```

Smart pointers are a powerful tool for managing resource lifetimes and avoiding common pitfalls with raw pointers.

5.2 Memory Pooling and Custom Allocators

For performance-critical applications, consider using memory pools or custom allocators to minimize the overhead of frequent allocations and deallocations.

5.2.1 Example Concept

Imagine you need to allocate many small objects repeatedly. Instead of calling new and delete each time, you can allocate a large block of memory and manage it manually. (Detailed implementation is beyond the scope of this chapter but is a valuable topic for further exploration.)

5.3 Best Practices in Memory Management

Initialize Pointers:

Always initialize pointers to nullptr and set them to nullptr after deleting.

Check for Memory Leaks:

Use tools like Valgrind to analyze your program for memory leaks.

RAII (Resource Acquisition Is Initialization):

Encapsulate resource management within classes so that resources are automatically released when objects go out of scope.

5.4 Code Optimization Techniques

Inline Functions:

Use the inline keyword for small functions to reduce call overhead.

Efficient Looping:

Optimize pointer arithmetic within loops to minimize overhead.

Avoiding Redundant Allocation:

Reuse allocated memory when possible instead of frequent allocation and deallocation.

By applying these advanced techniques, you can write code that is not only functionally correct but also highly efficient and scalable.

6. Troubleshooting and Problem-Solving

Even with a strong understanding of pointers and memory management, issues will arise. This section provides practical troubleshooting strategies for common problems.

6.1 Common Pitfalls

6.1.1 Dangling Pointers

A dangling pointer refers to memory that has been freed. Always set a pointer to nullptr after deleting its memory:

```cpp
delete ptr;
ptr = nullptr;
```

6.1.2 Memory Leaks

Failing to free memory leads to leaks. Tools like Valgrind can help identify leaked memory. Always ensure that every new has a corresponding delete.

6.2 Debugging Strategies

6.2.1 Compiler Warnings and Static Analysis

Enable compiler warnings (e.g., -Wall flag) to catch potential issues early. Use static analysis tools to examine your code for memory errors.

6.2.2 Using a Debugger

GDB is a powerful tool for stepping through your code, setting breakpoints, and inspecting pointer values. Compile with the -g flag to include debugging symbols, then run GDB to troubleshoot.

6.3   Real-World   Troubleshooting Examples

Consider a scenario where your Memory Puzzle Game crashes due to a segmentation fault. Steps to diagnose:

Reproduce the Issue:

Run the program under a debugger.

Inspect Pointers:

Check whether any pointers are nullptr or point to already freed memory.

Trace the Error:

Identify the exact line causing the crash.

Apply Fixes:

Ensure all dynamic memory is properly allocated and freed, and update pointers to nullptr after deletion.

By developing a systematic approach to troubleshooting, you not only resolve current issues but also build skills that prevent future problems.

7. Conclusion & Next Steps

As we conclude this chapter on pointers and memory management, let's review what you've learned and outline your next steps on the journey to mastering C++.

7.1 Recap of Key Points

Pointers and References:

You learned how pointers store memory addresses, how to perform pointer arithmetic, and how references serve as safer alternatives.

Dynamic Memory Allocation:

Using new and delete to allocate and free memory on the heap, and the importance of matching these operations to avoid leaks.

Project – Memory Puzzle Game:

You applied these concepts in a practical project that required dynamic memory management, reinforcing your understanding.

Advanced Techniques:

Topics such as smart pointers, custom memory management, and RAII were introduced to help you write efficient, leak-free code.

Troubleshooting:
Strategies for debugging memory errors and preventing common pitfalls were discussed.

7.2 Reflecting on Your Learning

Pointers and dynamic memory management are both powerful and complex. Every programmer encounters challenges with these topics, but each issue resolved is a significant step toward mastery. Reflect on the projects and examples in this chapter, and consider how these skills apply to larger, more complex systems.

7.3 Next Steps in Your C++ Journey

Practice:
Continue to experiment with pointers by implementing more complex data structures such as linked lists and trees.

Explore Further:

Study advanced memory management topics like smart pointers, custom allocators, and memory pooling.

Engage with the Community:

Participate in coding forums and open-source projects to learn from experienced developers and share your insights.

Further Reading:

Look for additional resources on memory management and modern C++ best practices.

7.4 Additional Resources

For further learning, consider these resources:

Books:

"Effective Modern C++" by Scott Meyers

"The C++ Programming Language" by Bjarne Stroustrup

Websites:

cppreference.com for comprehensive C++ documentation

LearnCPP.com for tutorials and exercises

Tools:

Valgrind for memory leak detection

GDB for debugging

7.5 Final Words of Encouragement

Mastering pointers and memory management is a challenging but essential part of becoming a proficient C++ programmer. Each new concept you learn opens up more possibilities for writing efficient, high-performance code. Embrace the challenges, keep experimenting, and remember that every error is an opportunity to learn.

CHAPTER 7: ADVANCED OBJECT-ORIENTED CONCEPTS

1 Introduction

In today's software landscape, object-oriented programming (OOP) is more than just a programming paradigm—it's a way of thinking about and organizing your code. In this chapter, we take a deeper dive into advanced OOP concepts: inheritance, polymorphism, encapsulation, and abstraction. These concepts empower you to write code that is modular, reusable, and scalable. You'll learn not only the "how" but also the "why" behind these principles, gaining insight into how they work together to form robust, maintainable systems.

Significance and Relevance

Imagine you're building a complex application such as a simulation of various vehicles—from cars to trucks, motorcycles, and buses. Without advanced OOP concepts, your code would quickly become tangled and hard to maintain. Inheritance allows you to define a general "Vehicle" class and then extend it for specific types, saving you time and reducing redundancy. Polymorphism enables your program to treat different vehicle types uniformly, even if their implementations differ. Encapsulation and abstraction hide the internal workings of your classes, making your code easier to understand and less prone to errors.

Understanding these concepts is essential for any C++ developer who wants to write efficient, maintainable software. Whether you're a beginner looking to expand your programming toolkit or a professional aiming to polish your skills, mastering advanced OOP techniques will open up new possibilities in your software projects.

Key Concepts and Terminology

Before we delve into the details, let's define some key terms:

Inheritance: The mechanism by which one class (the derived class) can inherit attributes and behaviors (methods) from another class (the base class). This promotes code reuse and establishes a hierarchical relationship.

Polymorphism: The ability of different classes to be treated as instances of the same class through a common interface, typically via virtual functions. It allows methods to behave differently based on the object's actual type.

Encapsulation: The bundling of data and the methods that operate on that data within a single unit or class, and restricting access to some of the object's components.

Abstraction: The concept of hiding the complex reality while exposing only the necessary parts. It helps in reducing programming complexity and effort.

Vehicle Hierarchy: A practical example that will be used throughout this chapter, where we model various types of vehicles using inheritance, polymorphism, encapsulation, and abstraction.

Setting the Tone

Throughout this chapter, our goal is to present these advanced concepts in a clear, approachable manner, using real-world analogies and practical examples. You will see how a well-designed class hierarchy can simplify your code, make it more flexible, and ultimately lead to better software design. We'll begin with an in-depth exploration of inheritance and polymorphism, then move on to encapsulation and abstraction. Finally, we'll tie everything together in our hands-on project: a Vehicle Hierarchy that simulates various vehicle types with differing behaviors.

Visual Aid: "Advanced OOP Overview" Diagram

[Diagram Description: A high-level flowchart depicting a base class labeled "Vehicle" with branches leading to derived classes such as "Car," "Truck," "Motorcycle," and "Bus." Each branch shows small icons representing unique characteristics (e.g., a car with four wheels, a truck with a trailer). Additional callouts highlight key OOP terms like inheritance, polymorphism, encapsulation, and abstraction.]

By the end of this chapter, you will have not only a theoretical understanding of advanced object-oriented concepts but also the practical skills to implement them in your own projects. Let's embark on this journey to master advanced OOP in C++.

2. Core Concepts and Theory

In this section, we explore the theoretical foundations of advanced object-oriented concepts. We will break down inheritance, polymorphism, encapsulation, and abstraction into easily digestible sub-sections, using analogies and real-world examples to illustrate these ideas. This will provide you with the conceptual tools needed to design robust class hierarchies and write modular, reusable code.

2.1 Inheritance: Building Upon Existing Code

Inheritance is a mechanism that allows one class (the derived or child class) to inherit attributes and behaviors from another (the base or parent class). This mechanism not only promotes code reuse but also facilitates a logical organization of code.

2.1.1 Basic Inheritance

Consider a simple example where we define a base class called Vehicle:

```cpp
#include <iostream>
#include <string>

using namespace std;

class Vehicle (
protected:
    string brand;
    int year;
public:
```

```cpp
    Vehicle(const string &brand, int year) : brand(brand),
year(year) ()
    virtual void displayInfo() const (
       cout << "Brand: " << brand << ", Year: " << year << endl;
    )
    virtual ~Vehicle() () // Virtual destructor for proper
cleanup in derived classes
);
```

Explanation:

The Vehicle class has common attributes like brand and year.

The constructor initializes these attributes.

The displayInfo() method outputs the vehicle's details.

A virtual destructor ensures that derived classes clean up correctly.

2.1.2 Derived Classes

Derived classes inherit from the base class and can extend or override its functionality. For example, a Car class may look like this:

```cpp
cpp
class Car : public Vehicle (
private:
    int numDoors;
public:
    Car(const string &brand, int year, int numDoors)
       : Vehicle(brand, year), numDoors(numDoors) ()
    void displayInfo() const override (
       Vehicle::displayInfo();
       cout << "Doors: " << numDoors << endl;
    )
);
```

Key Points:

The Car class inherits from Vehicle and adds a new attribute numDoors.

It overrides the displayInfo() method to include information about the number of doors.

2.1.3 Real-World Analogy

Think of inheritance like a family tree. A child inherits certain traits from their parents but can also have unique characteristics. In programming, the derived class inherits common features (attributes and methods) from the base class while adding or modifying behaviors specific to its role.

2.2 Polymorphism: One Interface, Multiple Forms

Polymorphism enables you to treat objects of different classes through a common interface. In C++, this is typically achieved via virtual functions.

2.2.1 Static vs. Dynamic Polymorphism

Static Polymorphism: Achieved through function overloading and templates, where the compiler determines which function to call at compile time.

Dynamic Polymorphism: Achieved through virtual functions, where the decision is made at runtime. This allows a base class pointer to call the appropriate derived class's method.

2.2.2 Virtual Functions and Overriding

Consider our earlier Vehicle example. By declaring displayInfo() as virtual in the base class and overriding it in derived classes, you enable dynamic polymorphism:

```cpp
void showVehicleInfo(const Vehicle &v) {
    v.displayInfo();
}
```

When you pass an instance of Car (or any derived class) to showVehicleInfo(), the correct version of displayInfo() is invoked based on the object's actual type.

2.3 Encapsulation and Abstraction: Hiding Complexity

2.3.1 Encapsulation

Encapsulation is the bundling of data and methods that operate on that data within a class, and restricting access to some of the object's components. This is achieved using access specifiers (private, protected, public).

Example:

```cpp
class Engine (
private:
    int horsepower;
public:
    Engine(int hp) : horsepower(hp) ()
    int getHorsepower() const ( return horsepower; )
    void setHorsepower(int hp) ( horsepower = hp; )
);
```

Encapsulation protects the internal state of an object and exposes only what is necessary. This minimizes dependencies and makes the code easier to maintain.

2.3.2 Abstraction

Abstraction is the process of hiding the complex implementation details of a system and exposing only the necessary parts. In C++, abstraction is achieved by designing classes that provide a simple interface for complex operations.

Example:

```cpp
class AbstractVehicle (
public:
    virtual void startEngine() = 0; // Pure virtual function
makes this an abstract class
    virtual ~AbstractVehicle() ()
```

);

Here, AbstractVehicle defines a common interface for vehicles without specifying how the engine is started. Derived classes provide the concrete implementation.

Real-World Analogy:

Consider a smartphone. You interact with its interface—tapping icons, swiping screens—without needing to understand the underlying hardware or software processes. Similarly, abstraction allows programmers to use complex functionality without delving into its intricate details.

2.4 How Advanced OOP Concepts Work Together

When combined, inheritance, polymorphism, encapsulation, and abstraction empower you to design flexible, scalable, and maintainable systems. For example, a vehicle hierarchy can start with an abstract Vehicle class that encapsulates common attributes and behaviors, which is then extended by more specific classes like Car, Truck, or Motorcycle that override and augment functionality as needed.

2.5 Summary of Core Theory

To summarize, this section has provided an in-depth look at:

Inheritance: How derived classes extend base classes to promote code reuse.

Polymorphism: The dynamic binding of methods to objects, enabling flexible interfaces.

Encapsulation: Protecting an object's internal state through controlled access.

Abstraction: Hiding complexity by exposing only essential features through interfaces.

With these advanced OOP principles firmly in place, you're ready to set up your environment and start implementing these ideas in real projects.

3. Tools and Setup

Before diving into hands-on examples, you need a properly configured development environment. In this section, we outline the necessary tools, platforms, and step-by-step instructions for setting up your environment to work with advanced object-oriented concepts in C++.

3.1 Selecting an Integrated Development Environment (IDE)

A robust IDE can significantly streamline the development process when working with advanced OOP concepts. Some popular options include:

Visual Studio Code (VS Code):

A lightweight, cross-platform editor enhanced with the C/C++ extension by Microsoft.

Code::Blocks:
An open-source IDE specifically designed for C++ programming, offering a straightforward interface ideal for beginners.

CLion:
A powerful IDE from JetBrains that provides advanced code analysis, refactoring tools, and integrated debugging.

Visual Studio (Windows):

A comprehensive environment with advanced debugging, profiling, and code navigation features.

Tip: For those new to C++ or advanced OOP, VS Code or Code::Blocks are highly recommended due to their ease of use and extensive community support.

3.2 Installing a C++ Compiler

C++ code must be compiled before execution. The most common compiler is GCC (GNU Compiler Collection), but you might also choose Clang or MSVC based on your platform.

For Windows: Installing MinGW (GCC)

Download MinGW-w64:

Visit MinGW-w64 and download the installer.

Install the Compiler:

Follow the installation instructions, ensuring that you select the C++ compiler.

Configure Environment Variables:

Add the path to the MinGW bin directory (e.g., C:\MinGW\bin) to your system's PATH.

Verify Installation:

Open Command Prompt and run:

```shell
g++ --version
```

For macOS: Installing Xcode Command Line Tools

Open Terminal:

Navigate to Applications > Utilities > Terminal.

Install Tools:

Run:

```shell
xcode-select --install
```

Verify Installation:

Run:

```shell
gcc --version
```

For Linux: Installing GCC

For Ubuntu or Debian-based distributions, run:

```shell
sudo apt update
sudo apt install build-essential
```

3.3 Configuring Your Project Workspace

Organize your project files in a clear directory structure. For our upcoming Vehicle Hierarchy project, you might structure your workspace as follows:

css

```
CppProjects/
└── VehicleHierarchy/
    ├── main.cpp
    ├── vehicle.h
    ├── vehicle.cpp
    ├── car.h
    ├── car.cpp
    ├── truck.h
    ├── truck.cpp
    └── motorcycle.h
       motorcycle.cpp
```

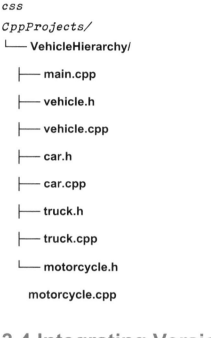

3.4 Integrating Version Control

Using Git for version control is highly recommended:

Install Git:

Download and install Git from git-scm.com.

Initialize a Repository:

Open your project directory and run:

shell

```
git init
```

Commit Regularly:

Regular commits help track changes and facilitate collaboration.

3.5 Verifying the Environment

Before implementing the Vehicle Hierarchy project, verify your setup by compiling a simple "Hello, World!" program that uses classes:

```cpp
#include <iostream>
using namespace std;

class Test (
public:
    void sayHello() const ( cout << "Hello, World!" << endl; )
);

int main() (
    Test t;
    t.sayHello();
    return 0;
)
```

Compile and run the program to confirm that your IDE, compiler, and version control are functioning correctly.

4. Hands-on Examples & Projects: Vehicle Hierarchy

This section is dedicated to practical application. We will build a Vehicle Hierarchy project that illustrates inheritance, polymorphism, encapsulation, and abstraction. The project simulates a variety of vehicles, each with its own characteristics, and demonstrates how advanced OOP concepts lead to flexible, maintainable code.

4.1 Project Overview

In the Vehicle Hierarchy project, you will:

Create a base class Vehicle that encapsulates common attributes and behaviors.

Derive specialized classes such as Car, Truck, and Motorcycle that override and extend the base functionality.

Use polymorphism to interact with different vehicle types through a common interface.

Demonstrate encapsulation by restricting access to internal data.

Implement abstraction by providing a clear, simple interface for complex operations.

4.2 Setting Up Project Files

Organize your project into several source files to maintain modularity. For example:

vehicle.h / vehicle.cpp: Base class declarations and definitions.

car.h / car.cpp: Derived class for cars.

truck.h / truck.cpp: Derived class for trucks.

motorcycle.h / motorcycle.cpp: Derived class for motorcycles.

main.cpp: Contains the main function and demonstrates polymorphism.

4.3 Implementing the Base Class: Vehicle

File: vehicle.h

```cpp
// vehicle.h: Declaration of the base Vehicle class
#ifndef VEHICLE_H
#define VEHICLE_H
```

```cpp
#include <string>
#include <iostream>

class Vehicle (
protected:
    std::string brand;
    int year;
public:
    Vehicle(const std::string &brand, int year);
    virtual void displayInfo() const;  // Virtual function
for polymorphism
    virtual ~Vehicle();            // Virtual destructor
);

#endif // VEHICLE_H
```

File: vehicle.cpp

```cpp
// vehicle.cpp: Definition of the base Vehicle class
#include "vehicle.h"

Vehicle::Vehicle(const std::string &brand, int year) :
brand(brand), year(year) ()

void Vehicle::displayInfo() const (
    std::cout << "Brand: " << brand << ", Year: " << year;
)

Vehicle:: ~Vehicle() (
    // Clean up resources if necessary
)
```

4.4 Implementing Derived Classes

4.4.1 Car Class

File: car.h

```cpp
// car.h: Declaration of the Car class derived from Vehicle
#ifndef CAR_H
#define CAR_H

#include "vehicle.h"

class Car : public Vehicle (
private:
    int numDoors;
public:
    Car(const std::string &brand, int year, int numDoors);
    void displayInfo() const override;
);

#endif // CAR_H
```

File: car.cpp

```cpp
// car.cpp: Definition of the Car class
#include "car.h"
#include <iostream>

Car::Car(const std::string &brand, int year, int numDoors)
    : Vehicle(brand, year), numDoors(numDoors) ()

void Car::displayInfo() const (
    Vehicle::displayInfo();
    std::cout << ", Doors: " << numDoors << std::endl;
)
```

4.4.2 Truck Class

File: truck.h

```cpp
// truck.h: Declaration of the Truck class derived from
Vehicle
#ifndef TRUCK_H
#define TRUCK_H

#include "vehicle.h"

class Truck : public Vehicle (
private:
    double loadCapacity;  // in tons
public:
    Truck(const std::string &brand, int year, double
loadCapacity);
    void displayInfo() const override;
);

#endif // TRUCK_H
```

File: truck.cpp

```cpp
// truck.cpp: Definition of the Truck class
#include "truck.h"
#include <iostream>

Truck::Truck(const std::string &brand, int year, double
loadCapacity)
    : Vehicle(brand, year), loadCapacity(loadCapacity) ()

void Truck::displayInfo() const (
    Vehicle::displayInfo();
```

```cpp
    std::cout << ", Load Capacity: " << loadCapacity << " tons"
<< std::endl;
)
```

4.4.3 Motorcycle Class

File: motorcycle.h

```cpp
// motorcycle.h: Declaration of the Motorcycle class
derived from Vehicle
#ifndef MOTORCYCLE_H
#define MOTORCYCLE_H

#include "vehicle.h"

class Motorcycle : public Vehicle (
private:
    bool hasSidecar;
public:
    Motorcycle(const std::string &brand, int year, bool
hasSidecar);
    void displayInfo() const override;
);
```

#endif // MOTORCYCLE_H

File: motorcycle.cpp

```cpp
// motorcycle.cpp: Definition of the Motorcycle class
#include "motorcycle.h"
#include <iostream>

Motorcycle::Motorcycle(const std::string &brand, int year,
bool hasSidecar)
    : Vehicle(brand, year), hasSidecar(hasSidecar) ()
```

```cpp
void Motorcycle::displayInfo() const (
    Vehicle::displayInfo();
    std::cout << ", Sidecar: " << (hasSidecar ? "Yes" : "No") <<
std::endl;
)
```

4.5 Main Program and Demonstrating Polymorphism

File: main.cpp

```cpp
cpp
// main.cpp: Demonstrates the Vehicle Hierarchy and
polymorphic behavior
#include <iostream>
#include <vector>
#include <memory> // For smart pointers
#include "vehicle.h"
#include "car.h"
#include "truck.h"
#include "motorcycle.h"


using namespace std;


int main() (
    // Create a vector of smart pointers to Vehicle objects
    vector<unique_ptr<Vehicle>> fleet;

    // Add various vehicles to the fleet
    fleet.push_back(make_unique<Car>("Toyota", 2020, 4));
    fleet.push_back(make_unique<Truck>("Volvo", 2018, 12.5));
```

```cpp
    fleet.push_back(make_unique<Motorcycle>("Harley-
Davidson", 2021, true));

    // Display information for each vehicle using
polymorphism
    cout << "Vehicle Fleet Information:" << endl;
    for (const auto &vehicle : fleet) {
        vehicle->displayInfo();
    }

    return 0;
}
```

Explanation:

We use a vector of smart pointers (unique_ptr) to manage our fleet, ensuring automatic memory management.

Each derived class is created and added to the vector.

A loop demonstrates polymorphism by calling the overridden displayInfo() method on each vehicle.

Visual Aid: "Vehicle Hierarchy Flow" Diagram

[Diagram Description: A diagram showing the vector holding pointers to objects of types Car, Truck, and Motorcycle, with arrows indicating polymorphic calls to the displayInfo() function on each object.]

4.6 Additional Exercises and Extensions

To further reinforce the concepts, try implementing these extensions:

Add More Vehicle Types:

Create additional classes such as Bus or SUV that derive from Vehicle and implement unique features.

Input from the User:

Allow users to input vehicle data and dynamically build the fleet.

Sorting and Filtering:

Implement functions to sort the vehicles by year or filter by brand.

GUI Integration:

Experiment with a graphical user interface using libraries like Qt to display the vehicle hierarchy visually.

5. Advanced Techniques & Optimization

In this section, we explore advanced techniques to further refine your object-oriented designs and optimize your code for performance and scalability.

5.1 Advanced Inheritance Strategies

5.1.1 Multiple Inheritance

C++ supports multiple inheritance, where a class can inherit from more than one base class. Use this feature with caution to avoid complexity.

Example Concept:

```cpp
cpp
class Amphibious (
public:
    virtual void driveOnLand() = 0;
    virtual void driveOnWater() = 0;
);


class AmphibiousCar : public Car, public Amphibious {
public:
    AmphibiousCar(const std::string &brand, int year, int numDoors)

        : Car(brand, year, numDoors) {}
```

```
void driveOnLand() override (
    std::cout << "Driving on land." << std::endl;
)
void driveOnWater() override (
    std::cout << "Driving on water." << std::endl;
)
);
```

5.1.2 Virtual Inheritance

When multiple inheritance leads to ambiguity (the "diamond problem"), virtual inheritance helps ensure that only one instance of a common base class is inherited.

5.2 Design Patterns for OOP

Familiarize yourself with common design patterns that leverage advanced OOP concepts:

Factory Pattern:

Create objects without specifying the exact class.

Strategy Pattern:

Define a family of algorithms, encapsulate each one, and make them interchangeable.

Observer Pattern:

Define a one-to-many dependency so that when one object changes state, all its dependents are notified.

5.3 Optimization Techniques

5.3.1 Code Refactoring

Keep your class hierarchies clean by refactoring code to remove redundancy and improve readability. Modularize functionality so that each class and function has a single responsibility.

5.3.2 Performance Considerations

Inlining Methods:

Use the inline keyword for small, frequently called functions.

Memory Management:

Leverage smart pointers to avoid leaks and reduce overhead.

Efficient Use of Polymorphism:

Understand the cost of virtual function calls and optimize hotspots accordingly.

5.4 Best Practices in Advanced OOP

Encapsulation and Data Hiding:

Even in complex hierarchies, ensure that internal data is hidden from external manipulation.

Use of Abstract Classes:
Define interfaces using pure virtual functions to enforce contracts.

Consistency in Naming and Structure:

Maintain a consistent coding style across your classes to make your codebase maintainable.

6. Troubleshooting and Problem-Solving

Advanced OOP code can be challenging to debug. In this section, we provide strategies to troubleshoot common issues encountered in inheritance, polymorphism, encapsulation, and abstraction.

6.1 Common Pitfalls

6.1.1 Virtual Function Issues

Missing   **Override:**
Ensure that overridden functions use the override keyword.

Improper Destruction:

Always declare a virtual destructor in base classes to prevent resource leaks.

6.1.2 Ambiguities in Multiple Inheritance

Diamond Problem:

Use virtual inheritance to avoid duplicate instances of the base class.

6.1.3 Access Specifier Mistakes

Encapsulation Breaches:

Verify that class members are appropriately marked as private, protected, or public.

6.2 Debugging Strategies

6.2.1 Compiler Warnings and Static Analysis

Compile with the -Wall flag to catch issues early and use static analysis tools to inspect your class hierarchies.

6.2.2 Using a Debugger

Step through your polymorphic calls with GDB or an IDE-integrated debugger. Check that the correct version of an overridden function is called.

6.3   Real-World   Example: Troubleshooting a Vehicle Hierarchy Issue

Imagine a scenario where a Car object is not displaying the correct number of doors. Steps to diagnose:

Verify Inheritance:

Check that Car::displayInfo() correctly calls Vehicle::displayInfo().

Check Data Members:

Ensure that numDoors is properly initialized.

Test with Multiple Vehicles:

Create instances of Car and other vehicles and verify polymorphic behavior.

6.4 Developing a Systematic Approach

Adopt a methodical approach to troubleshooting:

Isolate the Problem:

Create minimal examples to reproduce issues.

Consult Documentation:

Use resources like cppreference.com.

Collaborate:
Engage with communities (Stack Overflow, Reddit's r/cpp) for insights.

7. Conclusion & Next Steps

In this final section, we summarize the key points of advanced object-oriented programming and provide guidance on how to continue your journey.

7.1 Recap of Key Concepts

Inheritance and Polymorphism:

You learned how to build class hierarchies that promote code reuse and allow objects to be treated uniformly through base class pointers and virtual functions.

Encapsulation and Abstraction:

You explored how to protect internal state and hide complexity behind clear interfaces.

Project – Vehicle Hierarchy:

Through the Vehicle Hierarchy project, you applied advanced OOP concepts to create a flexible and scalable model of various vehicles.

Advanced Techniques:

We discussed multiple inheritance, virtual inheritance, design patterns, and performance optimizations.

Troubleshooting:
Strategies for debugging and solving common issues in advanced OOP were provided.

7.2 Reflecting on Your Learning

Advanced object-oriented concepts form the backbone of large-scale, maintainable software. As you reflect on what you've learned, consider how these techniques simplify complex problems by breaking them into manageable, modular pieces. Each design decision you make in your class hierarchy contributes to code that is easier to maintain, extend, and debug.

7.3 Next Steps in Your C++ Journey

Practice and Experiment:

Continue building projects that challenge you to design complex hierarchies. Experiment with multiple inheritance and abstract classes.

Deepen Your Understanding:

Explore additional design patterns and advanced topics such as template-based polymorphism.

Engage with the Community:

Share your projects, solicit feedback, and learn from the experiences of other developers.

Expand Your Toolkit:

Look into modern C++ features (C++11 and beyond) that further enhance OOP, such as lambda expressions and smart pointers.

7.4 Additional Resources

For further learning, consider these resources:

Books:

"Effective Modern C++" by Scott Meyers

"Design Patterns: Elements of Reusable Object-Oriented Software" by Erich Gamma, Richard Helm, Ralph Johnson, and John Vlissides

"The C++ Programming Language" by Bjarne Stroustrup

Websites:

cppreference.com for detailed documentation

LearnCPP.com for tutorials and exercises

Online Courses:

Look for courses that cover advanced OOP and design patterns.

7.5 Final Words of Encouragement

Mastering advanced object-oriented concepts is a challenging yet rewarding endeavor. Each project you build using inheritance, polymorphism, encapsulation, and abstraction will help solidify your understanding and prepare you for larger, more complex systems.

Embrace the iterative process of designing, coding, and debugging, and remember that every challenge is an opportunity to learn and grow.

Keep experimenting, seek out feedback, and continue to refine your skills. The knowledge you've gained in this chapter will serve as a cornerstone for your future projects and open doors to more advanced topics in software design.

CHAPTER 8: ADVANCED OBJECT-ORIENTED CONCEPTS

1 Introduction

In today's ever-evolving software landscape, object-oriented programming (OOP) remains one of the most powerful paradigms for managing complexity, promoting code reuse, and creating scalable applications. This chapter delves deep into advanced OOP concepts—specifically inheritance, polymorphism, encapsulation, and abstraction—and shows you how to leverage these principles to build a robust, flexible system. We will explore not only the theory behind these concepts but also their practical applications through a detailed project: the Vehicle Hierarchy.

Significance and Relevance

Imagine you are designing a software system for a transportation company that manages a diverse fleet of vehicles: cars, trucks, motorcycles, and buses. Without advanced OOP techniques, your code might become a tangled web of repeated logic and rigid structures that are difficult to maintain or extend. By applying advanced concepts like inheritance and polymorphism, you can create a base "Vehicle" class that encapsulates shared attributes and behaviors, and then derive specialized classes that override and extend that functionality. This not only reduces redundancy but also enhances scalability, as you can add new vehicle types with minimal changes to the existing code.

Similarly, encapsulation and abstraction allow you to hide internal implementation details and expose only the necessary interfaces to the rest of your application. This makes your code safer, easier to understand, and less prone to bugs.

Key Concepts and Terminology

Before diving in, let's define several key terms:

Inheritance: A mechanism that allows one class (derived) to inherit attributes and methods from another class (base), facilitating code reuse.

Polymorphism: The ability to treat objects of different classes through a common interface, particularly using virtual functions, so that the appropriate method is called based on the object's runtime type.

Encapsulation: The bundling of data and methods that operate on that data within a class, restricting access to some of the object's components.

Abstraction: The practice of exposing only the essential features of an object while hiding the complex implementation details.

Vehicle Hierarchy: A practical project example that models various vehicles using the aforementioned OOP concepts.

Setting the Tone

This chapter is structured to guide you from theoretical foundations to practical application. We start by exploring the core concepts, using real-world analogies and detailed code examples. Then, we move to tools and setup, ensuring that your development environment is configured for advanced C++ projects. Next, we immerse you in a hands-on project—the Vehicle Hierarchy—where you will implement inheritance, polymorphism, encapsulation, and abstraction in a concrete, engaging application. Finally, we cover advanced techniques, optimization strategies, troubleshooting tips, and conclude with guidance on next steps.

By the end of this chapter, you will not only understand advanced OOP concepts but also be able to apply them to create flexible and maintainable systems. Let's embark on this journey to master advanced object-oriented programming in C++.

2. Core Concepts and Theory

In this section, we break down the theoretical underpinnings of advanced object-oriented programming. We begin with inheritance and polymorphism, explaining how they allow you to build upon existing code and enable objects to be treated uniformly through a shared interface. We then explore encapsulation and abstraction—two critical principles that help hide complexity and protect your data. Throughout, we'll use analogies and real-world examples to illustrate these concepts.

2.1 Inheritance: Building Upon Existing Code

Inheritance allows a class (the derived class) to inherit attributes and behaviors from another class (the base class). This promotes code reuse and creates a natural hierarchy.

2.1.1 The Basics of Inheritance

Consider the following base class, Vehicle, which encapsulates common attributes such as brand and manufacturing year:

```cpp
#include <iostream>
#include <string>

class Vehicle (
protected:
    std::string brand;
    int year;
public:
    Vehicle(const    std::string    &brand,    int    year)    :
brand(brand), year(year) ()
    virtual void displayInfo() const (
        std::cout << "Brand: " << brand << ", Year: " << year;
    )
    virtual ~Vehicle() ()    // Virtual  destructor  to  allow
proper cleanup of derived classes
);
```

In this example, the Vehicle class provides a foundation upon which specialized vehicle types can be built. Notice the use of a virtual destructor, which is crucial when dealing with inheritance to ensure that derived class destructors are called correctly.

2.1.2 Derived Classes: Extending Functionality

Derived classes inherit from Vehicle and can add new attributes or override existing methods. For example, a Car class may introduce a new attribute—such as the number of doors—and override the displayInfo() method to include this detail:

```cpp
class Car : public Vehicle (
private:
    int numDoors;
public:
    Car(const std::string &brand, int year, int numDoors)
        : Vehicle(brand, year), numDoors(numDoors) ()
    void displayInfo() const override (
        Vehicle::displayInfo();
        std::cout << ", Doors: " << numDoors << std::endl;
    )
);
```

2.1.3 Real-World Analogy for Inheritance

Think of inheritance like a family tree: a child inherits traits from their parents yet can also have unique characteristics. Similarly, in programming, a derived class inherits common features from the base class while introducing its own specialized behavior.

2.2 Polymorphism: One Interface, Multiple Forms

Polymorphism allows you to treat objects of different types through a common interface. In C++, this is primarily achieved using virtual functions.

2.2.1 Understanding Dynamic Polymorphism

Dynamic polymorphism enables a base class pointer to refer to objects of derived classes and invoke the appropriate overridden function at runtime. Consider a function that displays vehicle information:

```cpp
void showVehicleInfo(const Vehicle &v) (
    v.displayInfo();
)
```

If you pass a Car object (or any derived class object) to showVehicleInfo(), the correct version of displayInfo() is called based on the object's actual type.

2.2.2 Static vs. Dynamic Polymorphism

Static Polymorphism: Achieved via function overloading and templates, resolved at compile time.

Dynamic Polymorphism: Achieved via virtual functions, resolved at runtime—offering greater flexibility when working with class hierarchies.

2.3 Encapsulation: Hiding Complexity

Encapsulation involves bundling data with the methods that operate on that data, and restricting direct access to some of the object's components. This protects the internal state and makes your code more modular.

2.3.1 Access Specifiers

In C++, encapsulation is enforced using access specifiers:

Private: Members are accessible only within the class.

Protected: Members are accessible within the class and its derived classes.

Public: Members are accessible from anywhere.

For example:

cpp

```
class Engine (
private:
    int horsepower;
public:
    Engine(int hp) : horsepower(hp) ()
    int getHorsepower() const ( return horsepower; )
    void setHorsepower(int hp) ( horsepower = hp; )
);
```

Real-World Analogy:

Consider a car's engine. The internal workings are hidden behind a cover (encapsulation), and you interact with the engine only through simple controls (methods).

2.4 Abstraction: Simplifying Complex Systems

Abstraction is the process of exposing only the essential features of an object while hiding the underlying complexity. In C++, abstraction is achieved through abstract classes and interfaces.

2.4.1 Abstract Classes

An abstract class is one that cannot be instantiated and typically contains one or more pure virtual functions. For example:

```cpp
cpp
class AbstractVehicle {
public:
    virtual void startEngine() = 0; // Pure virtual function
    virtual ~AbstractVehicle() ()
};
```

This forces derived classes to provide their own implementation of the startEngine() method, ensuring a consistent interface.

2.5 How Advanced OOP Concepts Work Together

When combined, inheritance, polymorphism, encapsulation, and abstraction provide a powerful framework for building flexible and maintainable software systems. They allow you to:

Reuse Code: Inheritance enables code reuse and minimizes redundancy.

Handle Diversity: Polymorphism allows different objects to be treated uniformly.

Protect Data: Encapsulation shields internal state from unintended interference.

Simplify Interfaces: Abstraction presents a simplified interface for complex systems.

2.6 Summary of Core Theory

In summary, this section has provided an in-depth look at:

Inheritance: Creating a class hierarchy to promote code reuse.

Polymorphism: Enabling objects to be used interchangeably through virtual functions.

Encapsulation: Protecting object state with access specifiers.

Abstraction: Hiding complexity through abstract classes and interfaces.

With these concepts in hand, you are ready to set up your development environment and build practical applications that demonstrate advanced OOP in action.

3. Tools and Setup

A proper development environment is critical for building advanced C++ projects. In this section, we outline the tools, platforms, and configuration steps necessary to effectively work with advanced OOP concepts.

3.1 Choosing an Integrated Development Environment (IDE)

For advanced OOP projects, a robust IDE can greatly enhance productivity. Some popular options include:

Visual Studio Code (VS Code):

A lightweight, cross-platform editor with powerful extensions for C++.

Code::Blocks:
An open-source IDE with a straightforward interface, ideal for beginners and intermediate developers.

CLion:
A professional IDE from JetBrains that offers advanced code analysis, refactoring, and debugging capabilities.

Visual Studio (Windows):
A comprehensive IDE with a feature-rich debugger and integrated project management tools.

Tip: For those new to advanced C++ development, VS Code or Code::Blocks are excellent choices due to their ease of use and extensive community support.

3.2 Installing a C++ Compiler

C++ code must be compiled into executable programs. The most commonly used compilers are GCC (GNU Compiler Collection) and Clang, with MSVC available on Windows.

For Windows: Installing MinGW (GCC)

Download MinGW-w64:

Visit MinGW-w64 and download the installer.

Install the Compiler:
Follow the installation instructions, ensuring that the C++ compiler is selected.

Configure Environment Variables:

Add the MinGW bin directory (e.g., C:\MinGW\bin) to your system's PATH.

Verify the Installation:

Open Command Prompt and run:

```shell
g++ --version
```
For macOS: Installing Xcode Command Line Tools

Open Terminal:

Navigate to Applications > Utilities > Terminal.

Install Tools:

Run:

shell
xcode-select --install
Verify the Installation:

Run:

shell
gcc --version
For Linux: Installing GCC

For Ubuntu or Debian-based systems:

shell
sudo apt update
sudo apt install build-essential

3.3 Configuring Your Project Workspace

Organize your project files in a clear, logical structure. For the Vehicle Hierarchy project, a recommended directory layout might be:

css

CppProjects/

└── **VehicleHierarchy/**

├── **main.cpp**

├── **vehicle.h**

├── **vehicle.cpp**

├── **car.h**

├── **car.cpp**

├── **truck.h**

├── truck.cpp

└── motorcycle.h

   motorcycle.cpp

3.4 Integrating Version Control

Using Git is essential for managing code changes and collaborating with others.

Install Git:

Download and install Git from git-scm.com.

Initialize a Repository:

In your project directory, run:

```shell
git init
```

Commit Your Code Regularly:

Regular commits help track changes and allow you to revert to previous states if necessary.

3.5 Verifying Your Environment

Before starting the main project, compile a simple test program that uses classes and virtual functions to ensure your environment is working properly:

```cpp
#include <iostream>
using namespace std;

class Test (
public:
    virtual void sayHello() const ( cout << "Hello, World!" <<
endl; )
```

```
);

int main() (
    Test t;
    t.sayHello();
    return 0;
)
```

Compile and run this program to confirm that your IDE, compiler, and debugging tools are functioning as expected.

4. Hands-on Examples & Projects: Vehicle Hierarchy

In this section, we apply the advanced OOP concepts discussed earlier by building a comprehensive Vehicle Hierarchy project. This project demonstrates inheritance, polymorphism, encapsulation, and abstraction in a real-world scenario.

4.1 Project Overview

The Vehicle Hierarchy project involves creating a system that models various types of vehicles. You will:

Develop a base class, Vehicle, which encapsulates common properties such as brand and manufacturing year.

Create derived classes like Car, Truck, and Motorcycle that inherit from Vehicle and introduce specialized attributes.

Utilize polymorphism to interact with different vehicle types through a unified interface.

Demonstrate encapsulation by protecting internal state and abstraction by exposing only necessary interfaces.

4.2 Setting Up Project Files

Organize your files as follows:

vehicle.h / vehicle.cpp: Base class definitions.

car.h / car.cpp: Definitions for the Car class.

truck.h / truck.cpp: Definitions for the Truck class.

motorcycle.h / motorcycle.cpp: Definitions for the Motorcycle class.

main.cpp: The driver program that demonstrates polymorphic behavior.

4.3 Implementing the Base Class: Vehicle

File: vehicle.h

```cpp
// vehicle.h: Declaration of the base Vehicle class
#ifndef VEHICLE_H
#define VEHICLE_H

#include <string>
#include <iostream>

class Vehicle (
protected:
    std::string brand;
    int year;
public:
    Vehicle(const std::string &brand, int year);
    virtual void displayInfo() const;  // Virtual function
for polymorphism
    virtual ~Vehicle();          // Virtual destructor
);


#endif // VEHICLE_H
File: vehicle.cpp
cpp
```

```cpp
// vehicle.cpp: Definition of the base Vehicle class
#include "vehicle.h"

Vehicle::Vehicle(const std::string &brand, int year) :
brand(brand), year(year) ()

void Vehicle::displayInfo() const (
    std::cout << "Brand: " << brand << ", Year: " << year;
)

Vehicle::~Vehicle() (
    // Cleanup, if necessary
)
```

4.4 Implementing Derived Classes

4.4.1 Car Class

File: car.h

cpp
```cpp
// car.h: Declaration of the Car class derived from Vehicle
#ifndef CAR_H
#define CAR_H

#include "vehicle.h"

class Car : public Vehicle (
private:
    int numDoors;
public:
    Car(const std::string &brand, int year, int numDoors);
    void displayInfo() const override;
);
```

```cpp
#endif // CAR_H
```
File: car.cpp

cpp

```cpp
// car.cpp: Definition of the Car class
#include "car.h"
#include <iostream>

Car::Car(const std::string &brand, int year, int numDoors)
    : Vehicle(brand, year), numDoors(numDoors) ()

void Car::displayInfo() const (
    Vehicle::displayInfo();
    std::cout << ", Doors: " << numDoors << std::endl;
)
```

4.4.2 Truck Class

File: truck.h

cpp
```cpp
// truck.h: Declaration of the Truck class derived from
Vehicle
#ifndef TRUCK_H
#define TRUCK_H

#include "vehicle.h"

class Truck : public Vehicle (
private:
    double loadCapacity; // in tons
public:
    Truck(const std::string &brand, int year, double
loadCapacity);
    void displayInfo() const override;
```

```cpp
);

#endif // TRUCK_H
```

File: truck.cpp

cpp

```cpp
// truck.cpp: Definition of the Truck class
#include "truck.h"
#include <iostream>

Truck::Truck(const std::string &brand, int year, double loadCapacity)
    : Vehicle(brand, year), loadCapacity(loadCapacity) ()

void Truck::displayInfo() const (
    Vehicle::displayInfo();
    std::cout << ", Load Capacity: " << loadCapacity << " tons" << std::endl;
)
```

4.4.3 Motorcycle Class

File: motorcycle.h

cpp

```cpp
// motorcycle.h: Declaration of the Motorcycle class derived from Vehicle
#ifndef MOTORCYCLE_H
#define MOTORCYCLE_H

#include "vehicle.h"

class Motorcycle : public Vehicle (
private:
    bool hasSidecar;
```

```cpp
public:
    Motorcycle(const std::string &brand, int year, bool
hasSidecar);
    void displayInfo() const override;
);
```

```cpp
#endif // MOTORCYCLE_H
File: motorcycle.cpp
cpp
```

```cpp
// motorcycle.cpp: Definition of the Motorcycle class
#include "motorcycle.h"
#include <iostream>

Motorcycle::Motorcycle(const std::string &brand, int year,
bool hasSidecar)
    : Vehicle(brand, year), hasSidecar(hasSidecar) ()

void Motorcycle::displayInfo() const (
    Vehicle::displayInfo();
    std::cout << ", Sidecar: " << (hasSidecar ? "Yes" : "No") <<
std::endl;
)
```

4.5 Main Program: Demonstrating Polymorphism

File: main.cpp

```cpp
cpp
// main.cpp: Demonstrates the Vehicle Hierarchy and
polymorphic behavior
#include <iostream>
#include <vector>
#include <memory> // For smart pointers
#include "vehicle.h"
#include "car.h"
```

```cpp
#include "truck.h"
#include "motorcycle.h"

using namespace std;

int main() {
    // Create a vector of smart pointers to Vehicle objects
    vector<unique_ptr<Vehicle>> fleet;

    // Add various vehicles to the fleet
    fleet.push_back(make_unique<Car>("Toyota", 2020, 4));
    fleet.push_back(make_unique<Truck>("Volvo", 2018, 12.5));
    fleet.push_back(make_unique<Motorcycle>("Harley-
Davidson", 2021, true));

    // Display information for each vehicle using
polymorphism
    cout << "Vehicle Fleet Information:" << endl;
    for (const auto &vehicle : fleet) {
        vehicle->displayInfo();
    }

    return 0;
}
```

4.6 Extensions and Exercises

To deepen your understanding, consider implementing these extensions:

Additional Vehicle Types:

Create further derived classes such as Bus or SUV with unique properties.

User Interaction:

Modify the program to allow user input for creating vehicles and dynamically building the fleet.

Sorting and Filtering:

Implement functionality to sort vehicles by year or filter by brand.

GUI Integration:

Experiment with a graphical interface using a library like Qt or SFML to display the vehicle information.

5. Advanced Techniques & Optimization

Once you are comfortable with building a basic Vehicle Hierarchy, you can further refine your design and optimize your code. This section covers advanced techniques and optimization strategies for working with complex class hierarchies and enhancing performance.

5.1 Advanced Inheritance Strategies

5.1.1 Multiple Inheritance

C++ allows classes to inherit from more than one base class. Although powerful, multiple inheritance can lead to complexity (e.g., the diamond problem). When using multiple inheritance, ensure you use virtual inheritance to avoid ambiguity.

5.1.2 Virtual Inheritance

To resolve the diamond problem (where a derived class inherits from two classes that both inherit from a common base), use virtual inheritance:

```cpp
class Base (
public:
    int value;
);

class Derived1 : virtual public Base ( );
```

```
class Derived2 : virtual public Base ( );

class Final : public Derived1, public Derived2 (
    // Only one instance of Base is present
);
```

5.2 Design Patterns and Best Practices

Familiarize yourself with common design patterns that leverage OOP principles:

Factory Pattern:

For creating objects without specifying the exact class.

Strategy Pattern:

For encapsulating algorithms and making them interchangeable.

Observer Pattern:

For establishing a one-to-many dependency between objects.

5.3 Optimization Techniques

5.3.1 Inlining Functions

For small, frequently called functions, use the inline keyword to reduce call overhead:

```cpp
inline int add(int a, int b) ( return a + b; )
```

5.3.2 Efficient Memory Management

Smart Pointers:

Continue using std::unique_ptr and std::shared_ptr to manage dynamic memory automatically.

Avoiding Redundancy:

Refactor your code to remove duplicate logic and reduce the number of virtual calls in performance-critical paths.

5.4 Code Refactoring and Maintenance

As your projects grow, keep your codebase maintainable:

Modularize:
Break your code into small, manageable functions and classes.

Consistent Naming:

Follow consistent naming conventions.

Documentation:
Maintain comprehensive comments and documentation for each class and method.

6. Troubleshooting and Problem-Solving

Advanced OOP projects can sometimes be challenging to debug. In this section, we discuss common pitfalls and provide strategies to troubleshoot issues related to inheritance, polymorphism, and memory management.

6.1 Common Issues

6.1.1 Virtual Function Pitfalls

Missing Override:

Always use the override keyword in derived classes to ensure that you are correctly overriding virtual functions.

Improper Destruction:

Ensure that base classes have a virtual destructor to prevent memory leaks when deleting derived objects through base pointers.

6.1.2 Ambiguity in Multiple Inheritance

Diamond Problem:

Use virtual inheritance to prevent duplicate instances of a common base class.

Access Conflicts:

Verify that access specifiers are correctly set to avoid unintentional exposure of internal data.

6.2 Debugging Techniques

6.2.1 Compiler Warnings and Static Analysis

Compile with flags such as -Wall to catch potential issues early. Use static analysis tools to inspect your code for design problems.

6.2.2 Step-by-Step Debugging

Utilize a debugger (GDB, Visual Studio Debugger) to step through your program, inspect variables, and verify that the correct overridden functions are being called.

6.3 Case Study: Troubleshooting a Vehicle Hierarchy Issue

Suppose a Car object isn't displaying the correct number of doors. To troubleshoot:

Check the Constructor:

Verify that the Car constructor initializes numDoors properly.

Verify Overriding:

Ensure that Car::displayInfo() calls Vehicle::displayInfo() and then outputs the door information.

Run Isolated Tests:

Create a minimal test case that instantiates a Car and calls displayInfo().

6.4 Developing a Systematic Approach

Adopt a methodical troubleshooting strategy:

Isolate the Issue:

Reduce the code to a minimal reproducible example.

Document Observations:

Keep a log of errors, warnings, and fixes.

Consult Resources:

Use online forums, documentation, and peers to gain insights.

7. Conclusion & Next Steps

In this final section, we summarize the advanced object-oriented concepts covered in this chapter and provide guidance for your continued learning journey.

7.1 Recap of Key Concepts

Inheritance and Polymorphism:

We explored how to build a hierarchy of classes using inheritance and how polymorphism enables you to interact with different derived classes through a common interface.

Encapsulation and Abstraction:

You learned how to protect internal state and expose only essential features, resulting in cleaner, more modular code.

Vehicle Hierarchy Project:

Through our hands-on project, you applied these concepts to create a flexible and extensible system that models various types of vehicles.

Advanced Techniques and Troubleshooting:

We covered strategies for handling complex inheritance scenarios, optimizing performance, and debugging common issues.

7.2 Reflecting on Your Learning

Advanced OOP concepts are the cornerstone of scalable and maintainable software. Reflect on how the Vehicle Hierarchy project illustrates the power of inheritance, polymorphism, encapsulation, and abstraction. Consider how these principles can be applied to your own projects, reducing complexity and improving code quality.

7.3 Next Steps in Your C++ Journey

Practice:
Continue building projects that challenge you to design complex class hierarchies. Experiment with multiple inheritance and abstract classes.

Deepen Your Knowledge:

Explore additional design patterns (such as Factory, Strategy, and Observer) that further leverage advanced OOP techniques.

Engage with the Community:

Participate in coding forums, contribute to open-source projects, and attend meetups to exchange ideas and get feedback.

Expand Your Toolkit:

Look into modern C++ features introduced in C++11 and later, such as lambda expressions, smart pointers, and move semantics, to further enhance your OOP skills.

7.4 Additional Resources

For further reading and practice, consider the following:

Books:

"Effective Modern C++" by Scott Meyers

"Design Patterns: Elements of Reusable Object-Oriented Software" by Gamma et al.

"The C++ Programming Language" by Bjarne Stroustrup

Websites:

cppreference.com for comprehensive documentation

LearnCPP.com **for tutorials and exercises**

Online Courses: Look for courses that focus on advanced C++ and design patterns to build on your newfound knowledge.

7.5 Final Words of Encouragement

Mastering advanced object-oriented concepts is challenging but immensely rewarding. As you continue to practice and refine your skills, you'll find that these techniques form the backbone of elegant, efficient, and maintainable software. Every project you complete, no matter how small, reinforces these principles and builds your confidence as a developer.

Keep exploring, experimenting, and pushing the boundaries of your knowledge. The advanced techniques you've learned in this chapter will serve as a solid foundation for tackling even more complex projects in the future.

CHAPTER 9: TEMPLATES AND THE STANDARD TEMPLATE LIBRARY (STL)

1. Introduction

In modern C++ programming, the concepts of templates and the Standard Template Library (STL) have transformed how developers write generic, reusable code. Whether you are a beginner or an experienced developer, mastering templates unlocks the power of generic programming—allowing you to write functions and classes that work with any data type without sacrificing performance. Meanwhile, the STL provides a rich set of pre-built data structures and algorithms that not only save time but also promote best practices in code design.

Why Templates and the STL Are Important

Imagine having to write multiple versions of the same function to handle integers, floats, or user-defined types. Without templates, you might have to duplicate code, leading to maintenance challenges and increased error risk. Templates allow you to write one function or class that adapts to any type, thereby promoting code reuse and reducing redundancy.

The STL, on the other hand, is a collection of well-tested classes and functions, such as vectors, lists, sets, maps, and algorithms (like sorting and searching), that provide the building blocks for almost every application. By using the STL, you can focus on solving the problem at hand rather than reinventing common data structures and algorithms.

Key Concepts and Terminology

In this chapter, we will cover:

Templates: A mechanism in C++ for creating generic functions and classes that work with any data type.

Generic Programming: Writing algorithms and data structures in a type-independent way.

The STL: A powerful library that includes containers (e.g., vector, list), iterators, algorithms, and function objects.

Generic Data Processor: A hands-on project that uses templates and the STL to process various data types generically.

Setting the Tone for the Journey

Our approach in this chapter is to combine theory with practice. We begin by laying a solid foundation in templates—explaining how they work and why they are so powerful. We then explore the STL, looking at how its containers and algorithms can be leveraged to solve real-world problems efficiently. Finally, you will implement a project, the Generic Data Processor, which will tie all these concepts together in a practical, engaging application.

By the end of this chapter, you will not only understand how to write generic code using templates but also how to use the STL to build powerful, efficient applications. Let's begin our journey into one of C++'s most powerful features.

2. Core Concepts and Theory

This section delves into the theoretical foundations of templates and the STL, breaking down the concepts into manageable parts. We begin with templates for generic programming, explore their syntax and usage, and then transition to the STL—covering its containers, iterators, algorithms, and function objects.

2.1 Introduction to Templates for Generic Programming

Templates allow you to write code without specifying exact data types. They make your code generic and reusable.

2.1.1 Function Templates

A function template defines a blueprint for a function. Here's an example that swaps two values:

```cpp
#include <iostream>
using namespace std;

// Function template for swapping two values
template <typename T>
void swapValues(T &a, T &b) {
    T temp = a;
    a = b;
    b = temp;
}

int main() {
    int x = 10, y = 20;
    cout << "Before swap: x = " << x << ", y = " << y << endl;
    swapValues(x, y);
    cout << "After swap: x = " << x << ", y = " << y << endl;

    double d1 = 1.5, d2 = 2.5;
    cout << "Before swap: d1 = " << d1 << ", d2 = " << d2 << endl;
    swapValues(d1, d2);
    cout << "After swap: d1 = " << d1 << ", d2 = " << d2 << endl;

    return 0;
}
```

Explanation:

The template keyword and typename T declare that the function works for any data type.

The function swapValues uses references to avoid ing data unnecessarily.

This template can be used to swap integers, doubles, or any type that supports assignment.

2.1.2 Class Templates

Class templates allow you to create generic classes. Consider a simple generic Pair class:

```cpp
#include <iostream>
using namespace std;

template <typename T1, typename T2>
class Pair (
public:
   T1 first;
   T2 second;
   Pair(T1 f, T2 s) : first(f), second(s) ()
   void display() const (
      cout << "Pair: (" << first << ", " << second << ")" <<
endl;
   )
);

int main() (
   Pair<int, double> p1(10, 3.14);
   p1.display();

   Pair<string, string> p2("Hello", "World");
   p2.display();

   return 0;
)
```

Key Points:

Class templates work similarly to function templates, but for classes.

They allow you to define data structures that are independent of the data type.

2.1.3 Benefits of Generic Programming

Code Reuse: Write one implementation that works for any type.

Type Safety: Errors are caught at compile time.

Performance: Templates allow inlining and other optimizations since they are resolved at compile time.

Real-World Analogy:

Think of a universal adapter that works with any plug. Just as you don't need a different adapter for every country, you don't need separate functions for every data type.

2.2 Exploring the Power of the STL

The Standard Template Library (STL) is a powerful collection of classes and functions that provide commonly used data structures and algorithms.

2.2.1 STL Containers

Containers are data structures that store collections of objects. Key containers include:

Vector: A dynamic array.

List: A doubly-linked list.

Deque: A double-ended queue.

Set and Multiset: Collections of unique elements, with set enforcing uniqueness.

Map and Multimap: Associative containers storing key-value pairs.

Example: Using a Vector

```cpp
#include <iostream>
#include <vector>
```

```cpp
using namespace std;

int main() {
    vector<int> numbers = {1, 2, 3, 4, 5};
    numbers.push_back(6);
    cout << "Vector elements: ";
    for (const int &num : numbers) {
        cout << num << " ";
    }
    cout << endl;
    return 0;
}
```

2.2.2 STL Iterators

Iterators act as pointers to traverse the contents of containers. They provide a uniform way to access container elements.

Example: Iterating with an Iterator

```cpp
cpp
#include <iostream>
#include <vector>
using namespace std;

int main() {
    vector<int> numbers = {10, 20, 30, 40, 50};
    for (vector<int>::iterator it = numbers.begin(); it != numbers.end(); ++it) {
        cout << *it << " ";
    }
    cout << endl;
    return 0;
}
```

2.2.3 STL Algorithms

The STL offers a variety of algorithms such as sort, find, and accumulate, which work seamlessly with STL containers.

Example: Using std::sort

```cpp
#include <iostream>
#include <vector>
#include <algorithm>
using namespace std;

int main() {
    vector<int> numbers = (50, 20, 40, 10, 30);
    sort(numbers.begin(), numbers.end());
    cout << "Sorted vector: ";
    for (int num : numbers) {
        cout << num << " ";
    }
    cout << endl;
    return 0;
}
```

2.2.4 STL Function Objects

Function objects (functors) are objects that can be used as though they were functions. They allow for stateful operations in algorithms.

Example: Custom Comparator Functor

```cpp
#include <iostream>
#include <vector>
#include <algorithm>
using namespace std;

struct Descending {
    bool operator()(int a, int b) {
        return a > b;
    }
};
```

```
int main() (
    vector<int> numbers = (10, 30, 20, 50, 40);
    sort(numbers.begin(), numbers.end(), Descending());
    cout << "Sorted in descending order: ";
    for (int num : numbers) (
        cout << num << " ";
    )
    cout << endl;
    return 0;
)
```

2.3 Integrating Templates and the STL

Templates and the STL go hand in hand. Templates allow you to create generic containers and algorithms, and the STL provides them ready to use. This synergy makes C++ a powerful language for generic programming.

Real-World Analogy:

Consider a Swiss Army knife that adapts to any situation. Templates provide the flexibility to create versatile tools, while the STL offers a set of pre-made, reliable tools that you can use immediately.

2.4 Summary of Core Concepts

This section has covered:

Templates: How to write generic functions and classes to enable code reuse.

STL Containers, Iterators, Algorithms, and Function Objects: How to leverage the STL to manage data efficiently.

Integration: How templates and the STL combine to make powerful, flexible code.

Armed with these theoretical foundations, you are now ready to set up your environment and start coding.

3. Tools and Setup

Before diving into hands-on examples, you must ensure that your development environment is configured correctly for working with templates and the STL. This section provides step-by-step instructions on selecting and setting up the right tools and platforms.

3.1 Choosing Your Development Environment

For advanced C++ projects, a feature-rich IDE can greatly improve your productivity. Consider these options:

Visual Studio Code (VS Code):

Lightweight and extensible with the Microsoft C/C++ extension.

Code::Blocks:
A straightforward, open-source IDE with built-in support for C++.

CLion:
A professional IDE from JetBrains, offering advanced refactoring and debugging tools.

Visual Studio (Windows):

A comprehensive IDE with integrated debugging and profiling tools.

Tip: For working with templates and the STL, choose an IDE that provides excellent code navigation and auto-completion features.

3.2 Installing a C++ Compiler

Your code must be compiled before it can run. The GCC compiler is widely used, but alternatives like Clang or MSVC are also popular.

For Windows: Installing MinGW (GCC)

Download MinGW-w64:

Visit MinGW-w64 and download the installer.

Installation:
Follow the installation wizard, ensuring that the C++ compiler is selected.

Configure PATH:

Add the MinGW bin directory (e.g., C:\MinGW\bin) to your system's PATH.

Verification:
Open Command Prompt and run:

```shell
g++ --version
```

For macOS: Installing Xcode Command Line Tools

Open Terminal:

Navigate to Applications > Utilities > Terminal.

Install Tools:

Run:

```shell
xcode-select --install
```

Verification:
Run:

```shell
gcc --version
```

For Linux: Installing GCC

For Ubuntu or Debian-based systems:

```shell
sudo apt update
sudo apt install build-essential
```

3.3 Configuring Your Project Workspace

Organize your project files with a clear directory structure. For the Generic Data Processor project, you might structure your workspace as follows:

css

CppProjects/

└── **GenericDataProcessor/**

├── **main.cpp**

├── **processor.h**

└── **processor.cpp**

3.4 Version Control Setup

Using Git for version control is highly recommended:

Install Git:

Download and install Git from git-scm.com.

Initialize a Repository:

In your project folder, run:

```shell
git init
```

Commit Regularly:

Frequent commits help track changes and facilitate collaboration.

3.5 Verifying Your Environment

Before moving on to the hands-on project, compile a simple test program that uses a template and an STL container:

```cpp
#include <iostream>
#include <vector>
using namespace std;

template <typename T>
```

```
void printVector(const vector<T>& v) (
    for (const T& item : v)
        cout << item << " ";
    cout << endl;
)


int main() (
    vector<int> numbers = (1, 2, 3, 4, 5);
    printVector(numbers);
    return 0;
)
```

Compile and run this program to ensure that everything is set up correctly.

4. Hands-on Examples & Projects: Generic Data Processor

In this section, you will apply templates and the STL in a practical project: the Generic Data Processor. This project is designed to process various types of data generically, demonstrating the power and flexibility of templates and the STL.

4.1 Project Overview

The Generic Data Processor is a console-based application that:

Uses templates to define functions that can process data of various types.

Leverages STL containers (like vectors and maps) to store and manipulate data.

Implements common operations such as sorting, filtering, and displaying data.

Provides a modular design that can be easily extended to support new data types and operations.

4.2 Setting Up the Project Files

Organize your project into the following files:

main.cpp: Contains the main function and user interaction loop.

processor.h: Declares the template functions and classes used for processing.

processor.cpp: Implements non-template functions (if any) and helper utilities.

4.3 Implementing the Template Functions

File: processor.h

```cpp
// processor.h: Declarations for the Generic Data Processor
#ifndef PROCESSOR_H
#define PROCESSOR_H

#include <vector>
#include <iostream>
#include <algorithm>
#include <functional>

// Template function to print elements of a container
template <typename T>
void printData(const std::vector<T>& data) {
    for (const auto& item : data)
        std::cout << item << " ";
    std::cout << std::endl;
}

// Template function to sort data in ascending order
template <typename T>
```

```cpp
void sortData(std::vector<T>& data) {
    std::sort(data.begin(), data.end());
}

// Template function to filter data based on a predicate
template <typename T, typename Predicate>
std::vector<T>   filterData(const   std::vector<T>&   data,
Predicate pred) {
    std::vector<T> result;
    for (const auto& item : data) {
        if (pred(item))
            result.push_back(item);
    }
    return result;
}

#endif // PROCESSOR_H
File: processor.cpp
cpp

// processor.cpp: Implementation file (if needed for non-
template functions)
// For template functions, definitions are included in the
header.
```

4.4 Implementing the Main Program

File: main.cpp

```cpp
cpp
// main.cpp: Main program for the Generic Data Processor
project
#include <iostream>
#include <vector>
```

```cpp
#include <string>
#include "processor.h"

using namespace std;

// Helper function to display a menu
void displayMenu() {
    cout << "\nGeneric Data Processor Menu:\n";
    cout << "1. Process Integers\n";
    cout << "2. Process Strings\n";
    cout << "3. Exit\n";
    cout << "Enter your choice: ";
}

int main() {
    int choice;
    bool running = true;

    while (running) {
        displayMenu();
        cin >> choice;

        switch (choice) {
            case 1: {
                // Processing integer data
                vector<int> intData = { 42, 7, 19, 23, 88, 15 };
                cout << "Original Integer Data: ";
                printData(intData);

                sortData(intData);
                cout << "Sorted Integer Data: ";
                printData(intData);

                // Filter: select integers greater than 20
```

```cpp
            auto filteredInts = filterData(intData, [](int x)
( return x > 20; ));
            cout << "Filtered Integer Data (x > 20): ";
            printData(filteredInts);
            break;
        )
        case 2: (
            // Processing string data
            vector<string> strData = ( "apple", "orange",
"banana", "kiwi", "grape" );
            cout << "Original String Data: ";
            printData(strData);

            sortData(strData);
            cout << "Sorted String Data: ";
            printData(strData);

            // Filter: select strings with length greater
than 5
            auto filteredStrs = filterData(strData, [](const
string &s) ( return s.length() > 5; ));
            cout << "Filtered String Data (length > 5): ";
            printData(filteredStrs);
            break;
        )
        case 3:
            running = false;
            cout << "Exiting Generic Data Processor.
Goodbye!" << endl;
            break;
        default:
            cout << "Invalid choice. Please try again." <<
endl;
    )
```

```
    )
    return 0;
)
```

Explanation:

printData: A template function to print any vector's contents.

sortData: Uses STL's std::sort to sort data.

filterData: Filters data based on a provided predicate (using a lambda function).

4.5 Testing and Extending the Project

After compiling and running the Generic Data Processor, test with both integer and string data. Consider the following extensions:

Additional Data Types:

Extend the processor to handle other types such as floating-point numbers.

Custom Objects:

Create a custom data type (e.g., a simple struct representing a record) and implement template functions to process a vector of these objects.

Enhanced Filtering:

Allow the user to input a custom filter condition at runtime.

4.6 Practical Applications

Templates and the STL are cornerstones of modern C++ programming. This Generic Data Processor project demonstrates how to build flexible, reusable code that can process data of any type. Such techniques are applicable in areas like:

Data analytics and processing pipelines

Database management systems

Scientific computing and simulations

5. Advanced Techniques & Optimization

After mastering the basics of templates and the STL, advanced techniques can further enhance performance and flexibility. This section explores best practices, optimization strategies, and advanced coding techniques that you can apply to your generic programming projects.

5.1 Advanced Template Techniques

5.1.1 Template Specialization

Sometimes, you may want to provide a custom implementation for a specific data type. This is achieved through template specialization.

```cpp
// General template for comparing two values
template <typename T>
bool isEqual(const T &a, const T &b) {
    return a == b;
}


// Template specialization for C-style strings (char arrays)
template <>
bool isEqual<const char*>(const char* const &a, const char* const &b) {
    return strcmp(a, b) == 0;
}
```

5.1.2 Variadic Templates

Variadic templates allow functions and classes to accept an arbitrary number of parameters. They are useful for creating flexible interfaces.

```cpp
#include <iostream>
using namespace std;
```

```cpp
template<typename... Args>
void printAll(Args... args) {
    ((cout << args << " "), ...);
    cout << endl;
}

int main() {
    printAll(1, 2.5, "Hello", 'A');
    return 0;
}
```

5.2 Advanced STL Techniques

5.2.1 Custom Comparators and Lambdas

Enhance STL algorithms by using custom comparators or lambda expressions to define specific sorting or filtering criteria.

```cpp
cpp
#include <iostream>
#include <vector>
#include <algorithm>
using namespace std;

int main() {
    vector<int> numbers = {10, 30, 20, 50, 40};
    sort(numbers.begin(), numbers.end(), [](int a, int b) {
        return a > b;  // Sort in descending order
    });
    for (int num : numbers) {
        cout << num << " ";
    }
    cout << endl;
    return 0;
```

)

5.2.2 Leveraging STL for Complex Data Structures

The STL is not just about vectors and arrays; containers like map, set, and unordered_map are invaluable for more complex data processing tasks. Understand when to use each container based on performance needs and usage patterns.

5.3 Optimization Strategies

5.3.1 Inlining and Code Bloat

For small, frequently called template functions, consider using the inline keyword to suggest inlining to the compiler. However, be mindful of code bloat if overused.

5.3.2 Memory and Performance Profiling

Use profiling tools (such as gprof or Valgrind) to identify bottlenecks in your template code or STL usage. Optimize based on profiling results, balancing speed and memory usage.

5.3.3 Compile-Time Computation

Templates allow for compile-time computations using techniques such as template metaprogramming. This can lead to significant performance improvements by moving computations from runtime to compile time.

5.4 Best Practices in Template Programming

Simplicity:
Avoid overly complex template logic. Keep your code readable and maintainable.

Documentation:
Document template parameters and intended usage clearly.

Error Handling:

Provide static assertions and clear error messages for misuse of templates.

Testing:
Write comprehensive tests to ensure that your generic code works correctly for all intended types.

6. Troubleshooting and Problem-Solving

(Approx. 1,000–1,500 words)

Working with templates and the STL can sometimes result in complex error messages and subtle bugs. This section provides strategies for troubleshooting and solving common issues encountered in generic programming.

6.1 Common Template Issues

6.1.1 Compilation Errors

Template-related compilation errors can be verbose. Common issues include:

Type Deduction Failures:

Ensure that your template parameters are deduced correctly.

Ambiguous Specializations:

Verify that specialized templates do not conflict with the general template.

Circular Dependencies:

Manage dependencies between template classes carefully.

6.1.2 STL-Related Issues

Iterator Invalidations:

Understand how operations like insertion and deletion affect iterators.

Algorithm Misuse:

Ensure that the algorithms you choose are appropriate for the container and data types involved.

6.2 Debugging Techniques

6.2.1 Compiler Warnings and Error Messages

Always compile with warnings enabled (e.g., -Wall -Wextra). Read the error messages carefully; they often provide clues on how to fix template-related issues.

6.2.2 Using a Debugger with Template Code

While debugging template code can be challenging, use debugging tools (GDB, Visual Studio Debugger) to step through instantiations and inspect the behavior of STL algorithms.

6.3 Troubleshooting the Generic Data Processor

For the Generic Data Processor project:

Verify Template Instantiation:

Ensure that the template functions are instantiated correctly for each data type.

Check STL Integration:

Validate that container operations (like sorting and filtering) are working as expected.

Run Isolated Tests:

Create small test cases for each template function to isolate and fix issues.

6.3.1 Before-and-After Example

Before:
A template function fails to compile due to a type mismatch.
After:
Adjust the function signature or add a type trait to ensure compatibility.

6.4 Developing a Systematic Troubleshooting Approach

Isolate and Simplify:

Reduce your code to a minimal example that reproduces the error.

Consult Documentation:

Use cppreference.com and other trusted sources for clarifications.

Engage with the Community:

Leverage forums like Stack Overflow for advice on complex template issues.

7. Conclusion & Next Steps

In this final section, we summarize the advanced topics covered in this chapter and outline the next steps for your journey in generic programming and the STL.

7.1 Recap of Key Concepts

Templates:
You learned how templates enable generic programming, allowing you to write functions and classes that operate with any data type.

STL:
The Standard Template Library provides a suite of containers, iterators, algorithms, and function objects that simplify data manipulation.

Integration:
By combining templates with the STL, you can write flexible, efficient, and reusable code.

Generic Data Processor Project:

This project demonstrated the practical application of these concepts, processing different types of data generically.

Advanced Techniques and Troubleshooting:

We explored template specialization, variadic templates, custom STL usage, and provided strategies for debugging and optimization.

7.2 Reflecting on Your Learning

Generic programming with templates and the STL is a game-changer in C++ development. It allows you to create highly reusable code that can adapt to various data types without sacrificing performance. Reflect on how the Generic Data Processor project exemplified these principles, and consider how you might apply them in your own projects—from data analysis tools to high-performance applications.

7.3 Next Steps in Your C++ Journey

Practice and Experiment:

Build more projects that use templates and the STL. Experiment with creating your own generic data structures and algorithms.

Deepen Your Knowledge:

Explore more advanced topics, such as template metaprogramming, and study design patterns that leverage generic programming.

Engage with the Community:

Participate in coding forums, attend workshops, and collaborate on open-source projects to gain new insights and feedback.

Keep Up with Modern C++:

Stay current with the latest C++ standards (C++11, C++14, C++17, C++20) as they continue to enhance generic programming capabilities.

7.4 Additional Resources

For further learning, consider these resources:

Books:

"Effective Modern C++" by Scott Meyers

"C++ Templates: The Complete Guide" by David Vandevoorde and Nicolai M. Josuttis

"The C++ Programming Language" by Bjarne Stroustrup

Websites:

cppreference.com for in-depth documentation and examples

LearnCPP.com **for tutorials and exercises**

Online Courses: Look for courses focusing on advanced C++ programming and generic programming techniques.

7.5 Final Words of Encouragement

Mastering templates and the STL opens up a new level of programming power in C++. The ability to write code that is both generic and efficient will serve you well throughout your development career. As you continue to experiment, refine your techniques, and build complex applications, remember that every challenge is an opportunity to deepen your understanding and improve your skills.

Keep pushing your boundaries, explore new ideas, and don't be afraid to experiment with advanced template techniques. Your journey into generic programming has just begun, and the tools and strategies you've learned in this chapter will be invaluable in your future projects.

CHAPTER 10: MODERN C++ FEATURES

1. Introduction

Modern C++ has evolved dramatically over the past decade. With the introduction of C++11 and subsequent standards like C++14, C++17, and C++20, the language has grown to become more expressive, efficient, and easier to use. In this chapter, we explore the modern features that set contemporary C++ apart from its predecessors. We'll discuss the enhancements introduced in the newer standards, such as lambda expressions, the auto keyword, range-based for loops, smart pointers, and much more. These features not only simplify coding but also help you write safer, more efficient, and maintainable code.

Why Modern C++ Matters

Imagine rewriting legacy software with new requirements while ensuring your code is both backward-compatible and forward-looking. Modern C++ provides the tools to modernize your codebase, make it more robust, and improve its performance. Whether you're a beginner eager to learn current best practices or a professional looking to update older code, understanding modern C++ is essential. With its powerful features, you can write generic, efficient, and elegant code that is easier to debug and extend over time.

Key Concepts and Terminology

In this chapter, we will cover:

C++11 to C++20 Enhancements: An overview of key new features from each standard.

Lambda Expressions: Anonymous functions that enable inline function definitions.

The Auto Keyword: Automatic type deduction that simplifies variable declarations.

Modern Iteration and Ranges: Enhanced loops and range-based operations.

Smart Pointers and Move Semantics: Tools for safer and more efficient memory management.

Project – Refactoring Legacy Code: A hands-on project that demonstrates how to modernize an existing codebase using modern C++ features.

Setting the Tone

Our goal is to provide a balanced mix of theory and practical application. We begin by outlining the evolution of modern C++ features and explaining why they matter. Then, we'll dive into detailed discussions of lambda expressions, the auto keyword, and other modern constructs. Finally, you'll put your knowledge into practice by refactoring a sample legacy code project, transforming it into a modern, efficient, and maintainable codebase.

By the end of this chapter, you will have a deep understanding of the new features that have reshaped C++, and you'll be equipped to refactor legacy code using these modern tools. Let's begin our journey into the exciting world of Modern C++.

2. Core Concepts and Theory

This section delves into the theoretical foundations of modern C++ features introduced from C++11 through C++20. We break down these concepts into several key areas: an overview of the enhancements, a deep dive into lambda expressions and the auto keyword, and discussions on other modern improvements that streamline programming and improve performance.

2.1 Overview of C++11 to C++20 Enhancements

Modern C++ is defined by a series of language standards that have each introduced significant improvements:

2.1.1 C++11

Lambda Expressions: Allow you to write inline, anonymous functions.

Auto Keyword: Enables automatic type deduction.

Smart Pointers: std::unique_ptr, std::shared_ptr for safer memory management.

Range-Based For Loops: Simplify iteration over containers.

Move Semantics: Allow efficient resource transfer, reducing unnecessary ing.

2.1.2 C++14 and C++17

Relaxed Lambda Capture: More flexible lambda expressions.

Structured Bindings: Decompose objects into individual variables.

If constexpr: Compile-time conditional statements.

Parallel Algorithms: Enhance performance with multithreading support in STL algorithms.

2.1.3 C++20

Concepts: Constraints on template parameters for clearer generic programming.

Modules: A new way to organize code and manage dependencies.

Coroutines: Facilitate asynchronous programming.

Ranges Library: Provides composable range views and actions for working with sequences of data.

2.2 Using Lambda Expressions

Lambda expressions enable you to create anonymous functions on the fly. They are particularly useful for short, inline operations, especially in conjunction with STL algorithms.

2.2.1 Syntax and Basics

A basic lambda expression in C++ looks like this:

```cpp
auto lambda = ()() (
    std::cout << "Hello from lambda!" << std::endl;
```

```cpp
);
lambda();
```

Explanation:

[] indicates the start of a lambda.

Parentheses () contain parameters (which can be omitted for none).

Curly braces {} contain the function body.

The lambda is assigned to a variable using auto for type deduction.

2.2.2 Capturing Variables

Lambdas can capture variables from their surrounding scope:

```cpp
int factor = 2;
auto multiply = (factor)(int x) (
    return x * factor;
);
std::cout << multiply(5); // Outputs 10
```

You can capture variables by value or by reference, providing flexibility in how the lambda interacts with its environment.

2.2.3 Practical Examples with Lambdas

Lambda expressions are especially powerful when used with STL algorithms. For example, you can use a lambda to filter elements in a vector:

```cpp
#include <iostream>
#include <vector>
#include <algorithm>
using namespace std;

int main() (
    vector<int> numbers = (1, 2, 3, 4, 5, 6);
    vector<int> evenNumbers;
```

```cpp
    // only even numbers using a lambda as a predicate
    _if(numbers.begin(),                          numbers.end(),
back_inserter(evenNumbers), ()(int x) (
        return x % 2 == 0;
    ));

    cout << "Even numbers: ";
    for (int num : evenNumbers) (
        cout << num << " ";
    )
    cout << endl;
    return 0;
)
```

2.3 Using the Auto Keyword

The auto keyword allows automatic type deduction, simplifying variable declarations and making code more concise and easier to read.

2.3.1 Basic Usage

Instead of explicitly specifying a type, you can let the compiler deduce it:

```cpp
cpp
auto x = 42;        // x is an int
auto y = 3.14;      // y is a double
auto z = "Hello";   // z is a const char*
```
2.3.2 In Function Declarations and Ranges

auto is particularly useful with STL containers and iterators:

```cpp
cpp
#include <iostream>
#include <vector>
using namespace std;
```

```cpp
int main() {
    vector<int> vec = (10, 20, 30);
    for (auto it = vec.begin(); it != vec.end(); ++it) {
        cout << *it << " ";
    }
    cout << endl;
    return 0;
}
```

It also works well with range-based for loops, reducing boilerplate:

cpp

```cpp
for (auto num : vec) {
    cout << num << " ";
}
```

2.3.3 Benefits and Considerations

Improved Readability:

Reduces clutter in code by eliminating repetitive type names.

Maintenance:
Makes code easier to update if data types change.

Caution:
Overuse of auto can sometimes obscure the code's intent. Use it where it improves clarity.

2.4 Integrating Modern C++ Features

Modern C++ features like lambda expressions and the auto keyword work seamlessly with the STL. They allow for cleaner, more expressive code that can be written more quickly and maintained more easily.

Real-World Analogy:

Imagine replacing a bulky, manual tool with a sleek, automated device that adapts to any task. Lambda expressions and auto are such tools in modern C++—they make your code lighter, more flexible, and easier to work with.

2.5 Summary of Core Concepts

To recap, this section has covered:

The evolution of modern C++ features from C++11 through C++20.

How lambda expressions provide a concise way to write inline functions.

The power of the auto keyword in reducing verbosity and enhancing maintainability.

The seamless integration of these features with the STL to create elegant and efficient code.

Armed with these modern tools, you are now ready to modernize existing codebases. In the next section, we will cover the tools and setup needed to begin refactoring legacy code.

3. Tools and Setup

Before you start refactoring legacy code using modern C++ features, you need to ensure your development environment is configured correctly. This section details the tools and setup required for a smooth transition to modern C++.

3.1 Selecting an IDE or Text Editor

For modern C++ development, a robust IDE can significantly enhance productivity:

Visual Studio Code (VS Code):

Lightweight and highly extensible with excellent support for modern C++ via the Microsoft C/C++ extension.

CLion:
A powerful IDE from JetBrains offering advanced refactoring, debugging, and code analysis tools.

Visual Studio:

A comprehensive IDE on Windows with strong support for modern C++ standards.

Code::Blocks:
An open-source IDE that is simple to use and effective for C++ projects.

Tip: Choose an IDE that supports modern C++ standards and provides features such as auto-completion, code navigation, and refactoring tools.

3.2 Installing a Modern C++ Compiler

Modern C++ features require a compiler that supports C++11 and beyond. Popular compilers include:

GCC:
Ensure you have version 5.0 or later.

Clang:
A modern compiler with excellent support for C++ standards.

MSVC:
Visual Studio's compiler that supports modern C++ features.

For Windows: Installing MinGW-w64 (GCC)

Download:
Visit MinGW-w64 and download the installer.

Install:
Follow the installation wizard and select a recent version.

Configure PATH:

Add the compiler's bin directory (e.g., C:\MinGW\bin) to your system PATH.

Verify:
Open Command Prompt and run:

shell

g++ —version

For macOS and Linux

Follow similar installation steps using package managers or by downloading the latest compiler from official repositories.

3.3 Configuring Your Project Workspace

Organize your project directory to support refactoring legacy code. For the Generic Data Processor project (or a sample legacy code project), a recommended structure might be:

css

CppProjects/

└── LegacyCodeRefactor/

  ├── main.cpp

  ├── legacy.h

  ├── legacy.cpp

  ├── modern.h

  └── modern.cpp

This structure helps you separate legacy code from new, refactored code.

3.4 Integrating Version Control

Using Git is essential for managing code changes during refactoring:

Install Git:

Download from git-scm.com.

Initialize a Repository:

Run git init in your project folder.

Commit Regularly:

Commit your changes often to track progress and facilitate rollback if needed.

3.5 Verifying Your Environment

Test your setup by compiling a simple program that uses modern C++ features:

```cpp
#include <iostream>
#include <vector>
using namespace std;

int main() {
    auto nums = std::vector<int>(1, 2, 3, 4, 5);
    for (auto num : nums) {
        std::cout << num << " ";
    }
    std::cout << std::endl;
    return 0;
}
```

Compile and run this program to confirm that your environment is ready for modern C++ development.

4. Hands-on Examples & Projects: Refactoring Legacy Code

In this section, we apply modern C++ features to a real-world project: refactoring a piece of legacy code. This project, titled **Refactoring Legacy Code**, demonstrates how to modernize an old codebase using lambda expressions, the auto keyword, and other modern constructs.

4.1 Project Overview

Legacy code can be difficult to maintain and extend due to outdated practices and verbose syntax. In this project, you will:

Identify a segment of legacy code that uses old-style C++ (pre-C++11).

Refactor the code to leverage modern C++ features such as lambda expressions, auto, range-based for loops, and smart pointers.

Compare the legacy and refactored versions to highlight improvements in readability, performance, and maintainability.

4.2 Analyzing Legacy Code

Consider a simple legacy code snippet that processes a list of numbers:

```cpp
#include <iostream>
#include <vector>
using namespace std;

int main() (
    vector<int> nums;
    for (int i = 0; i < 5; i++) (
        nums.push_back(i * 10);
    )
    for (vector<int>::iterator it = nums.begin(); it != nums.end(); ++it) (
        cout << *it << " ";
    )
    cout << endl;
    return 0;
)
```

Issues with the Legacy Code

Verbose Type Declarations:

Explicit iterator types clutter the code.

Traditional For Loops:

More modern constructs can simplify iteration.

Lack of Modern Constructs:

No use of lambda expressions or auto for type deduction.

4.3 Refactoring Using Modern C++ Features

Let's refactor the above legacy code to make it more concise and modern.

4.3.1 Using the Auto Keyword and Range-Based For Loop

```cpp
#include <iostream>
#include <vector>
using namespace std;

int main() {
    vector<int> nums;
    for (int i = 0; i < 5; i++) {
        nums.push_back(i * 10);
    }
    // Modern range-based for loop with auto for type deduction
    for (auto num : nums) {
        cout << num << " ";
    }
    cout << endl;
    return 0;
}
```

Benefits:

The iterator type is deduced automatically.

The range-based loop is more concise and easier to read.

4.3.2 Incorporating Lambda Expressions

Suppose you want to process the vector to filter out values above a threshold. In legacy code, you might write a loop with conditionals; using lambdas and STL algorithms simplifies the process:

```cpp
```

```cpp
#include <iostream>
#include <vector>
#include <algorithm>
using namespace std;

int main() {
    vector<int> nums = {10, 20, 30, 40, 50};
    // Use a lambda to count numbers greater than 25
    int count = count_if(nums.begin(), nums.end(), [](int x)
{ return x > 25; });
    cout << "Count of numbers > 25: " << count << endl;
    return 0;
}
```

4.3.3 Using Smart Pointers for Memory Management

Legacy code often uses raw pointers, which can be error-prone. Modern C++ encourages the use of smart pointers:

cpp

```cpp
#include <iostream>
#include <memory>
using namespace std;

class Data {
public:
    int value;
    Data(int val) : value(val) {}
};

int main() {
    // Using a unique_ptr for automatic memory management
    unique_ptr<Data> ptr = make_unique<Data>(100);
    cout << "Value: " << ptr->value << endl;
```

```
return 0;
}
```

4.4 Integrating Refactored Code into a Larger Legacy System

In a more comprehensive refactoring project, you might:

Replace raw pointers with smart pointers.

Use auto and range-based for loops throughout the code.

Introduce lambda expressions to replace small helper functions.

Modularize the code by breaking monolithic functions into smaller, templated, or lambda-based functions.

4.5 Hands-on Walkthrough: A Complete Refactoring Project

Imagine a legacy module that processes data records in an inefficient manner. In the refactored version:

Input Module:

Use modern file I/O libraries and smart pointers.

Data Processing:

Use STL algorithms combined with lambda expressions for filtering and transformation.

Output Module:

Use range-based for loops to display processed data.

Example Refactored Code Outline:

```cpp
#include <iostream>
#include <vector>
```

```cpp
#include <string>
#include <algorithm>
#include <memory>
#include <fstream>

using namespace std;

// A legacy data record structure
struct Record {
    string name;
    int value;
};

// Modern function to process records
void processRecords(vector<Record>& records) {
    // Sort records by name using a lambda
    sort(records.begin(), records.end(), [](const Record& a,
const Record& b) {
        return a.name < b.name;
    });
    // Filter records with value greater than 50
    auto it = remove_if(records.begin(), records.end(), [](const
Record& r) {
        return r.value <= 50;
    });
    records.erase(it, records.end());
}

// Modern function to display records
void displayRecords(const vector<Record>& records) {
    for (const auto& record : records) {
        cout << record.name << ": " << record.value << endl;
    }
}
```

```
int main() (
    // Suppose legacy code read records into a raw array; we
use a vector instead
    vector<Record> records = (("Alice", 30), ("Bob", 60),
("Charlie", 80), ("Dave", 45));
    processRecords(records);
    displayRecords(records);
    return 0;
)
```

4.6 Testing and Validation

After refactoring, rigorous testing is essential. Create unit tests to validate that:

The refactored code produces the same (or improved) results.

Memory management is robust, with no leaks (use tools like Valgrind).

The codebase is easier to extend with additional features.

5. Advanced Techniques & Optimization

Once you've refactored legacy code using modern C++ features, you can further optimize and enhance your code. This section discusses advanced techniques and optimization strategies.

5.1 Template Metaprogramming and Compile-Time Computation

Modern C++ allows certain computations to be performed at compile time using templates. This can improve performance by reducing runtime overhead.

Example: Computing Factorial at Compile Time

cpp

```
template <int N>
struct Factorial (
    static const int value = N * Factorial<N - 1>::value;
);

template <>
struct Factorial<0> (
    static const int value = 1;
);

int main() (
    std::cout << "Factorial of 5: " << Factorial<5>::value <<
std::endl;
    return 0;
)
```

5.2 Optimizing Lambda Usage

When lambdas are used in performance-critical code:

Capture Minimization:

Capture only what is necessary to reduce overhead.

Inlining Lambdas:

Modern compilers often inline lambdas, but you can use hints when needed.

5.3 Advanced STL Optimization

Leverage advanced STL techniques:

Custom Allocators:

Use custom memory allocators for STL containers to optimize memory usage.

Parallel Algorithms (C++17):

Use parallelized versions of algorithms for performance improvements on multi-core systems.

5.4 Best Practices in Modern Code Optimization

Profile Before Optimizing:

Use tools like gprof or Visual Studio's profiler to understand where improvements are needed.

Balance Readability and Performance:

While optimization is important, maintain clear, readable code.

Refactor Incrementally:

Optimize small sections at a time and test thoroughly.

6. Troubleshooting and Problem-Solving

As with any major refactoring or adoption of modern features, you may encounter challenges. This section outlines common issues and practical troubleshooting strategies.

6.1 Common Issues with Modern C++ Features

6.1.1 Lambda Expression Pitfalls

Capture Defaults:

Be mindful of capturing by value versus by reference.

Compiler Errors:

Modern compilers often provide detailed error messages for lambda issues. Read them carefully.

6.1.2 Auto Keyword Misuse

Overuse:
Excessive use of auto may obscure the code's intent.

Type Deduction Errors:

Ensure that auto deduces the intended type, particularly in complex expressions.

6.1.3 Refactoring Legacy Code

Behavioral Changes:

Confirm that refactored code maintains the original functionality.

Memory   **Leaks:**
Use memory analysis tools to ensure that modern memory management practices are correctly implemented.

6.2 Debugging Modern C++ Code

6.2.1 Compiler Warnings

Compile with all warnings enabled (e.g., -Wall -Wextra) to catch issues early.

6.2.2 Step-by-Step Debugging

Use debugging tools (GDB, Visual Studio Debugger) to step through refactored code, checking that modern constructs behave as expected.

6.3 Case Studies and Before-and-After Examples

Present examples of legacy code alongside refactored modern code. Discuss the challenges encountered and the solutions implemented.

Example: Legacy Loop vs. Range-Based Loop

Before:

```cpp
for (std::vector<int>::iterator it = vec.begin(); it != vec.end(); ++it) {
    // Process *it
}
```

After:

```cpp

for (auto num : vec) {
    // Process num
}
```

Discuss improvements in readability and maintenance.

6.4   Systematic   Problem-Solving Strategies

Isolate Problems:

Reduce code to minimal examples.

Consult Documentation:

Use reliable sources like cppreference.com.

Peer Review:

Engage with the community to gather insights.

7. Conclusion & Next Steps

In this final section, we summarize the key takeaways from this chapter and outline the next steps to further your mastery of modern C++ features.

7.1 Recap of Key Concepts

Modern C++ Enhancements:

We reviewed the major improvements from C++11 to C++20 that have modernized the language.

Lambda Expressions and Auto:

These features simplify code, reduce boilerplate, and improve readability.

STL Integration:

The STL continues to be a cornerstone for efficient data manipulation.

Refactoring Legacy Code:

The Generic Data Processor project demonstrated how to modernize an existing codebase using modern C++ features.

Advanced Techniques and Optimization:

We discussed strategies to further optimize modern C++ code and best practices for debugging and troubleshooting.

7.2 Reflecting on Your Learning

Modern C++ offers powerful tools that enable you to write code that is more concise, efficient, and easier to maintain. The transition from legacy coding practices to modern techniques not only improves performance but also prepares your code for future challenges. Reflect on how the use of lambda expressions, the auto keyword, and advanced STL features can simplify your day-to-day coding tasks and reduce errors.

7.3 Next Steps in Your C++ Journey

Practice Regularly:

Continue to experiment with modern C++ features by refactoring additional legacy codebases or creating new projects.

Deepen Your Knowledge:

Explore advanced topics such as template metaprogramming, concurrency with C++20, and further STL enhancements.

Community Engagement:

Participate in forums, contribute to open-source projects, and attend conferences or local meetups focused on modern C++.

Keep Up with Standards:

Stay current with evolving C++ standards to continually refine your skills and incorporate new best practices.

7.4 Additional Resources

For further study, consider these resources:

Books:

"Effective Modern C++" by Scott Meyers

"C++ Concurrency in Action" by Anthony Williams

"The C++ Programming Language" by Bjarne Stroustrup

Websites:

cppreference.com for comprehensive reference material.

LearnCPP.com for tutorials and hands-on exercises.

Online Courses: Seek courses that focus on modern C++ programming and advanced design patterns.

7.5 Final Words of Encouragement

Embracing modern C++ features is an ongoing journey that transforms not just the way you write code, but also how you think about problem-solving and software design. Every improvement—from using lambdas to refactoring legacy code—contributes to writing cleaner, more efficient, and more maintainable programs. As you move forward, remember that continuous learning and practice are the keys to mastery. The techniques you have learned in this chapter will empower you to write future-proof code that can evolve with changing technology.

Happy coding, and may your journey into modern C++ be filled with discovery, efficiency, and lasting success!

CONCLUSION

Recap of Key Concepts

Throughout this chapter, we have embarked on an in-depth exploration of modern C++ features that have fundamentally transformed the language over the past decade. Let's take a moment to revisit the major topics we covered:

Modern C++ Enhancements (C++11 to C++20):

We began by examining the evolution of the language from C++11 through C++20. Each new standard brought with it significant improvements that modernized C++—from enhanced performance and better memory management to more expressive syntax and powerful abstractions. Key milestones included the introduction of lambda expressions, the auto keyword, smart pointers, range-based for loops, structured bindings, concepts, modules, and coroutines. These features have not only made C++ more powerful but have also streamlined the development process, making code safer and easier to maintain.

Lambda Expressions:

One of the most exciting additions to modern C++ is the ability to define anonymous functions using lambda expressions. We learned how lambdas can simplify code by enabling you to write inline functions for short tasks without the overhead of separate function definitions. Whether filtering data with STL algorithms or creating quick, one-off callbacks, lambdas offer a concise and expressive syntax that can greatly reduce boilerplate and improve clarity.

The Auto Keyword:

The auto keyword has revolutionized how we write variable declarations. By allowing the compiler to deduce the type of a variable, auto reduces redundancy and the risk of errors from manual type specification. We saw how auto can simplify code, particularly when dealing with complex STL container types or iterators, thereby enhancing both readability and maintainability.

The Standard Template Library (STL):

We delved into the STL, a cornerstone of modern C++ programming. The STL's comprehensive collection of containers, iterators, algorithms, and function objects enables you to manipulate data efficiently and elegantly. We discussed how using STL not only saves time by eliminating the need to write common data structures from scratch but also promotes best practices through well-tested, optimized code.

Refactoring Legacy Code:

Perhaps one of the most practical aspects of modern C++ is its ability to breathe new life into legacy code. Our hands-on project, the Generic Data Processor, demonstrated how modern features—such as lambda expressions, auto, and enhanced STL capabilities—can be used to refactor and modernize an outdated codebase. This transformation not only improves performance but also makes the code more understandable and maintainable for future development.

Advanced Techniques and Optimization:

We also touched upon advanced techniques, including template specialization, variadic templates, and compile-time computations. These strategies allow you to push the boundaries of generic programming and optimize your code for both speed and memory efficiency. With these tools, you can write code that is both highly abstracted and incredibly performant.

Resources for Continued Learning

Your journey with modern C++ doesn't end here. To continue expanding your knowledge and mastering these powerful features, consider the following resources:

Books:

"Effective Modern C++" by Scott Meyers: A must-read for understanding how to write efficient, modern C++ code.

"C++ Templates: The Complete Guide" by David Vandevoorde and Nicolai M. Josuttis: This book offers an in-depth look at templates and generic programming.

"The C++ Programming Language" by Bjarne Stroustrup: Written by the creator of C++, this book provides a comprehensive overview of the language and its evolution.

"Modern Effective C++" (if available): Look for new editions or complementary texts that explore the latest C++ standards and best practices.

Online References and Documentation:

cppreference.com: An indispensable resource for up-to-date C++ documentation and examples.

LearnCPP.com: A highly accessible tutorial site that covers both basic and advanced C++ topics.

Official ISO C++ website: Offers news, proposals, and resources related to the evolving standards.

Communities and Forums:

Stack Overflow: A vibrant community where you can ask questions, share knowledge, and learn from experienced developers.

Reddit's r/cpp: Engage with discussions, insights, and shared projects from a community passionate about C++.

Local Meetups and Conferences: Attend events like CppCon, ACCU, or regional C++ meetups to network with peers, attend workshops, and stay abreast of the latest trends.

GitHub: Explore open-source projects written in modern C++ to see how experienced developers apply these techniques in real-world scenarios.

Online Courses and Tutorials:

Platforms such as Coursera, Udemy, and Pluralsight offer courses on modern C++ programming. Look for courses specifically focused on C++11 and later standards, as well as topics like advanced templates, lambda expressions, and the STL.

YouTube channels dedicated to C++ programming can also provide visual explanations and practical coding sessions.

Blogs and Articles:

Many experienced C++ developers share insights and tutorials on personal blogs. Regularly reading articles can keep you updated on best practices and emerging trends in the C++ community.

Final Words of Encouragement

Embarking on the journey to master modern C++ is both challenging and immensely rewarding. The concepts and tools we've explored in this chapter—

lambda expressions, the auto keyword, the STL, and advanced techniques for refactoring legacy code—are not just features of a language; they are powerful instruments that empower you to write clean, efficient, and maintainable code.

Here are a few parting thoughts to inspire you as you continue your journey:

Embrace the Change:

Transitioning from legacy C++ to modern C++ can seem daunting, but each new feature you adopt will streamline your code and open up new possibilities. Embrace these tools as they are designed to simplify your work and enhance your productivity.

Practice Consistently:

Mastery of modern C++ comes from consistent practice. Refactor old projects, experiment with new features, and build fresh ones. Every challenge you face is an opportunity to learn and grow.

Stay Curious and Open-Minded:

The world of C++ is vast and continually evolving. Keep exploring new standards and techniques, and never hesitate to dive deep into topics that pique your interest. The more you learn, the more you will be able to innovate and solve complex problems.

Learn from the Community:

The C++ community is full of passionate developers who are eager to share their knowledge. Engage with others, ask questions, contribute to open-source projects, and participate in discussions. Collaboration and shared learning are vital to your success.

Celebrate Progress:

Every small improvement in your code, every bug you fix, and every new feature you master is a milestone in your journey. Celebrate these successes— they are the building blocks of your expertise.

Remember, modern C++ is not just about writing code—it's about writing code that lasts, code that evolves, and code that inspires others. The principles and practices you've learned here will serve as the foundation for a career in software development that is both exciting and fulfilling.

APPENDICES

1. Glossary of Terms

Abstraction:
The process of hiding complex implementation details and exposing only the necessary parts of an object or system. Abstraction simplifies user interaction with code by providing a clear interface.

Auto Keyword:

A feature introduced in C++11 that allows the compiler to automatically deduce the type of a variable from its initializer. This reduces verbosity and makes code easier to maintain.

C++11, C++14, C++17, C++20:

Different versions of the C++ language standard. Each introduces new features and enhancements. For example, C++11 introduced lambda expressions and auto, while C++20 brought concepts and modules.

Compiler:
A program that translates C++ source code into machine code. Common compilers include GCC, Clang, and MSVC.

Encapsulation:
A principle of object-oriented programming that combines data and the methods that operate on that data into a single unit (a class), restricting direct access to some of the object's components.

Generic Programming:

A programming paradigm in which algorithms are written in terms of types to-be-specified-later that are then instantiated when needed for specific types. Templates are the primary tool for generic programming in C++.

Inheritance:
A mechanism in which a new class (derived class) is created from an existing class (base class), inheriting attributes and behaviors, which promotes code reuse and hierarchical organization.

Lambda Expression:

An anonymous function defined directly in the code, often used for short tasks. Lambdas are especially useful in conjunction with STL algorithms for concise, inline operations.

Legacy Code:

Older code written using outdated practices or language standards. Modern C++ techniques can be applied to refactor legacy code, making it more efficient, readable, and maintainable.

Polymorphism:

The ability of different classes to be treated as instances of the same class through a common interface. In C++, polymorphism is typically achieved via virtual functions, allowing for dynamic method binding at runtime.

Range-Based For Loop:

A simplified syntax for iterating over the elements of a container introduced in C++11. It enhances readability by abstracting away iterator details.

Smart Pointers:

Template classes in the STL (such as std::unique_ptr and std::shared_ptr) that provide automatic memory management by ensuring that dynamically allocated memory is properly freed.

Standard Template Library (STL):

A collection of C++ template classes and functions that provide commonly used data structures (e.g., vectors, lists, maps) and algorithms (e.g., sort, find) to simplify data manipulation and improve code reuse.

Template:

A feature in C++ that allows functions and classes to operate with generic types. Templates are the foundation of generic programming, enabling code reuse without sacrificing type safety.

Type Deduction:

The process by which the C++ compiler automatically determines the type of a variable or expression, often used in conjunction with the auto keyword and templates.

2. Additional Resources and Tools

Books

"Effective Modern C++" by Scott Meyers
A comprehensive guide on how to use modern C++ features effectively.

"C++ Templates: The Complete Guide" by David Vandevoorde and Nicolai M. Josuttis

An in-depth look at template programming, providing both theoretical and practical insights.

"The C++ Programming Language" by Bjarne Stroustrup
Written by the creator of C++, this book covers the language in detail.

"Modern Effective C++" (if available)

Look for new editions that focus on best practices in modern C++.

Online References and Documentation

cppreference.com:
A comprehensive online reference for C++ language features and the STL.

https://en.cppreference.com

LearnCPP.com:
A free, structured tutorial site covering both basic and advanced C++ topics.
https://www.learncpp.com

ISO C++ Website:

Offers news, proposals, and resources related to the C++ standards.
https://isocpp.org

Communities and Forums

Stack Overflow:

A vibrant community where you can ask questions and learn from experienced developers.

Reddit's r/cpp:

A community of C++ enthusiasts discussing best practices, challenges, and new developments.

Local Meetups and Conferences:

Look for events like CppCon, ACCU, or local C++ user groups to network and share knowledge.

Tools and IDEs

Visual Studio Code (VS Code):

A lightweight, cross-platform editor with powerful extensions for C++.

CLion:
A feature-rich IDE from JetBrains with advanced refactoring and debugging tools.

Visual   Studio:
A comprehensive IDE with robust support for modern C++ standards.

Code::Blocks:
An open-source IDE that is beginner-friendly and effective for C++ projects.

Compilers:

GCC: Ensure you have version 5.0 or later for full modern C++ support.

Clang: A modern alternative known for its expressive error messages.

MSVC: The Microsoft Visual C++ compiler, integrated with Visual Studio.

Online Courses and Tutorials

Coursera,   Udemy,   and   Pluralsight:
These platforms offer courses specifically focused on modern C++ features and advanced programming techniques.

YouTube Channels:

Channels like "TheCherno" and "Bo Qian" provide video tutorials on modern C++ programming.

GitHub:
Explore repositories with modern C++ projects to see how others apply these concepts in real-world scenarios.

3. Coding Conventions and Style Guides

Adhering to coding conventions and style guides is essential for producing clean, readable, and maintainable code. Below are some widely adopted standards and best practices for C++:

General Conventions

Consistent Naming:

Use **camelCase** or **snake_case** consistently across your project.

Class names typically start with an uppercase letter (e.g., Vehicle, DataProcessor).

Variable and function names should be descriptive and start with a lowercase letter (e.g., calculateTotal, numItems).

Indentation and Spacing:

Use 2 or 4 spaces per indentation level consistently.

Keep lines of code within 80–100 characters where possible.

Place braces on the same line as the statement they belong to, or follow your team's style if different.

Comments and Documentation

Inline Comments:

Use inline comments to explain non-obvious parts of your code. Avoid over-commenting trivial lines.

Documentation Comments:

Use tools like Doxygen to create documentation from your source code. Write clear documentation for classes, functions, and parameters.

Block Comments:

Use block comments to separate major sections of code or to provide an overview of complex functions.

File and Project Organization

Modularization:
Organize code into logical units—use separate header (.h) and source (.cpp) files for class definitions and implementations.

Directory Structure:

Maintain a clear directory structure for your project. For example:

```
php

ProjectName/

├── include/      // Header files

├── src/        // Source files

├── tests/       // Unit tests

└── docs/        // Documentation
```

Modern C++ Specific Guidelines

Use of Modern Features:

Embrace modern C++ constructs such as lambda expressions, the auto keyword, range-based for loops, and smart pointers.

Avoid Raw Pointers:

Prefer smart pointers (std::unique_ptr, std::shared_ptr) for dynamic memory management.

Const Correctness:

Declare variables and member functions as const where applicable to prevent unintended modifications.

Error Handling:

Use exceptions or error codes consistently. Provide meaningful error messages and use RAII (Resource Acquisition Is Initialization) to manage resources.

Popular Style Guides

Google C++ Style Guide:

A widely recognized style guide that provides comprehensive rules and recommendations for writing C++ code. Google C++ Style Guide

LLVM Coding Standards:

Used by the LLVM project, these guidelines are another solid reference for modern C++ practices. LLVM Coding Standards

C++ Core Guidelines:

Developed by Bjarne Stroustrup and others, these guidelines offer best practices and recommendations for modern C++. C++ Core Guidelines

Tools for Enforcing Style

Clang-Format:
A tool that automatically formats your C++ code according to a predefined style guide.

Cppcheck:
A static analysis tool that helps detect bugs and enforce coding standards.

IDE Plugins:

Many IDEs offer plugins or built-in features to enforce coding conventions and style consistency.

www.ingramcontent.com/pod-product-compliance
Lightning Source LLC
LaVergne TN
LVHW052128070326
832902LV00039B/4125